Developing Summary and Note-taking Skills

Third edition (revised)

Marian Barry

Contents

Introduction		iv
Science and the body		**2**
Note-taking 1	Tackling dyslexia in children	2
Summary 1	All in the mind?	4
Note-taking 2	Antibiotic resistance	6
Summary 2	The enemy within	8
Animal life		**10**
Note-taking 3	The thrill of watching whales	10
Summary 3	Why zoo cats lose their cool	12
Note-taking 4	The secret world of polar bears	14
Summary 4	Undercover cats	16
The world of plants		**18**
Note-taking 5	A natural antiseptic	18
Summary 5	The rose, queen of all flowers	20
Note-taking 6	Sweet talk	22
Summary 6	The mangoes in your trolley	24
Personal challenges		**26**
Note-taking 7	Lost on the mountain	26
Summary 7	Young ambassadors	28
Note-taking 8	Taking a gap year	30
Summary 8	My daughter can achieve whatever she wants	32
Leisure and lifestyle		**34**
Note-taking 9	The ugly side of clean power	34
Summary 9	From schoolboy to clown	36
Note-taking 10	The world of the Incas	38
Summary 10	What's for dinner, Mum?	40
Trends – past, present and future		**42**
Note-taking 11	Birth of a barcode	42
Summary 11	Pupils find internet 'a poor learning tool'	44
Note-taking 12	Thirsty work	46
Summary 12	Lost for words	48

Skills practice: Core level — 50
Note-taking 13	The Huron-Wendat	50
Summary 13	Travel writer	52
Note-taking 14	The rise of the robot	54
Summary 14	Laughter: the best medicine	56

Skills practice: Extended level — 58
Note-taking 15	The Huron-Wendat	58
Summary 15	Serval rescue	60
Note-taking 16	The rise of the robot	62
Summary 16	Space mission	64

Topic vocabulary and writing tasks — 66
Acknowledgements — 114
Teacher's Notes (with answers edition only) — 115
Answer key (with answers edition only) — 119

Introduction

About this book

The purpose of this book is to help you develop effective note-taking skills and the ability to write concise summaries based on a range of interesting reading texts. As you progress through your course, you will find that both of these skills will be important in order to further your knowledge and understanding of texts and your interpretation of them. The book has been updated for the 2019 syllabus where the marks for notes and summaries can help contribute towards the marks allocated in an answer.

Taking good notes and writing summaries are important for personal as well as academic reasons. Being confident in these skills will benefit you in your other school subjects and may help contribute to higher levels of success overall.

The basic skills you will learn from this book will start you off in the right way for future success too. Once you have acquired the correct methods, your study skills can be extended and improved for use on a degree course, in training and in careers when you may need to take notes at meetings or give presentations.

I believe you already have many of these skills, possibly without knowing you have them. For example, your friends might want to know what happened in a film you recently watched. If you give them an outline of the story, you are giving them a 'summary'.

Themes

There are six themed (topic) sections – Science and the body, Animal life and so on. If you are already familiar with some of the themes from your school subjects, that is great, but if not, do not worry as you do not need special knowledge to understand the topics. The themed sections alternate note-taking exercises with summary exercises.

Note-taking

You will take a set of notes based on the reading text and there are multiple points for you to find about each text. The headings and bullet points given for each exercise are to help you to choose the correct information from the text. In all note-taking exercises, one mark has been allocated for each correct bullet point you find. In the practice exercises, (note-taking 1–12) you will notice that there are more points to find and note down than in the core and extended sections. This is to provide you with as much opportunity as possible to practice this skill before moving onto the exam-style note-taking activities in note-taking 13–16.

Summary

You will write a summary paragraph based on the text you have read, using some of your own words. You will practise choosing the correct information for the question and keeping to a word limit of 100 words (and not more than 120 words). Across these exercises, the summary is worth 16 marks and is marked for both correct content points (8 marks) and good use of language (8 marks).

Skills builder

The note-taking exercises are followed by a 'Skills builder' where you practise writing a connected paragraph based on your notes. It is a practical way of learning how the brief notes you have already made can be developed into full sentences and linked together well. Marks are allocated here for both language use (8 marks) and content points (8 marks).

Tip

Each exercise has a 'Tip' with information and advice to help you succeed.

Skills practice

These two sections later in the book are divided into Skills practice Note-taking and Summary exercises for the Core and Extended levels. Here you will find a series of exercises to stretch your learning and challenge you to put into practice the skills you have developed throughout the book. You can try these any time when you feel you are ready. You may also find them a useful tool to help you prepare for examinations.

Topic vocabulary

These words and phrases are to help you build up your vocabulary. The language comes from the texts you studied in order to write your notes and summaries. At the bottom of the page, you will see a 'Vocabulary challenge', which is an interesting way for you to check your understanding and ability to apply the words and expressions in the vocabulary groups given above.

Writing tasks

The vocabulary section ends with composition questions for you to practise your writing skills. You should refer to the Topic vocabulary feature to help create suitable sentences for your compositions.

Tips and strategies

Reading strategies

Before you begin to read a passage, it is a good idea to prepare your mind for the task. Don't rush into reading.

- Look at the question, headings and pictures.
- Make sure you understand the question and underline key words. The key words are important, so discuss with a friend whether you both agree on what they actually are.
- Use the information to guess what the text might be about. This will help you start correctly. For example, the note-taking exercise called 'Antibiotic resistance'. Check what this means by asking questions, sharing ideas with friends or looking in a dictionary. You can then discuss how antibiotic resistance might affect the way sick people get treatment in the future.
- If you have explored a topic already, in science lessons perhaps, use what you know, as it will benefit you.
- When you read the text, read actively. Underline interesting facts, for example, with a pencil.
- Check any vocabulary that confused you, but remember you don't need to understand every word in a text to understand it well.
- After reading, discuss the text in your group. Ask questions about ideas you did not fully understand or give your opinion on ideas in the text.
- You can then start to answer the question, using the tried and tested methods below.

A tried and tested method for note-taking

1 Read the question carefully and underline the key words as you read.

2 Look carefully at the heading, and at any pictures or photos in order to pick up extra clues about the content before you begin to read the text.

3 Read the text fairly quickly, with as much concentration as possible. Slow down and reread any parts you find

confusing during first reading. Don't worry if you still don't understand a bit of the text. Persevere and continue reading, because you may need to read through the complete text before you understand the different bits properly. Reread the text a second time if necessary.

4 Underline key parts of the text that are relevant to the question as soon as you notice them.

5 Then complete any bullet points or numbered points by copying short, relevant words and phrases from the text, or using words of your own. You do **not** need to write complete sentences.

Be selective and don't just copy out large parts of the original text. Remember, you are making notes, not writing paragraphs. Your completed notes should be brief, concise and easily understood, even by someone who has not seen the original text.

A tried and tested method for summary writing

Use the above method as far as step 4.

5 Draft a rough paragraph from the key words and phrases, using sentences. Use your own words as much as you can. You do not need to change specialised terms and technical words.

6 Count the number of words you have written. Make corrections to the grammar and spelling if necessary, and add any linking words to make your paragraph flow more smoothly.

7 Write a final draft in about 100 words (and not more than 120 words). If you find you do not have time to write out a neat final copy then making clear corrections to the first draft, such as altering punctuation, putting in a linking word or correcting grammar, is quite acceptable and well worth doing.

Writing better summaries

- Use the tried and tested method above.
- Don't add any views of your own. All the facts and opinions should come from the text.
- Use some words of your own to show a wide vocabulary.
- Start some sentences with a different word or introductory expression. For example, if you are writing a summary about polar bears, don't always begin each sentence with the words polar bears. Consider reorganising the whole sentence sometimes so as to achieve a more varied style.
- Use linking words (for example: moreover, nevertheless, also, in addition) to join ideas together.
- Avoid writing lots of very short sentences.
- Write more concisely. Can you use one word or expression for example, instead of giving a list? *Spoons, teaspoons, knives, forks* could be replaced by the single word *cutlery*.
- Check your grammar and aim to be accurate in tenses and word order.
- Check your punctuation. Start each sentence with a capital letter and end with a full stop. Use apostrophes to show possession and if you have left a letter out. Use commas to separate words in a list.

Avoiding common mistakes

- Make sure you read, understand and underline the key words for the questions, so you start correctly. For example, in a question about the achievements of the Inca civilisation, information in the text about the food they ate and the language they spoke is not relevant because eating and talking are not achievements.
- For notes, check you understand the key words in headings. Make sure you put the correct information under the correct heading. For example, in a question about treating children who have dyslexia, the information about daily eye exercises belongs to the heading 'Treatment **after** the tests' and not to the previous heading about treatment **during** the tests.
- Find a separate piece of information for each bullet point in the notes. Remember to reread your work to make sure you have not repeated the same information. If you have repeated yourself, you will need to reread the heading and locate different information in the text to match the heading.
- In the text, the main point can be expressed in a variety of ways without adding anything genuinely new to

the main point. For example, the question may ask you to find the reason why a polar bear uses underground shelter. The main point for you to locate is that the polar bear needs to protect themselves. Write that point down and you will get one mark. Other words in the text such as *frightened*, *trapped*, *hostile* and *threatened* expand on the idea, but the information given is not different enough to make another main point. If you add these ideas, you will still only get one mark. This book gives you a lot of practice in developing skills in these challenging aspects of summarising and note-taking.

- Copying a true fact from the text that has no relevance to the actual question is a frequent mistake. One way to resolve it is to look closely at the question again to see what exactly it is looking for. Next, compare the key words in the question with the answer you have written. Make the necessary changes.
- Copying large parts of the text is also a common mistake. Your notes should be brief and relevant. If you are writing summaries, select the main points only and try to use some of your own words.

Writing compositions

Take a few moments to prepare to write. Don't rush into writing.

- First, highlight the key words in the question.
- Make a simple outline plan.
- Choose the most suitable words and phrases from the topic vocabulary list to develop the plan.
- Aim for three main paragraphs, plus an introductory sentence and a closing sentence.
- Think about who you are writing to: is it a formal report for the headteacher or an informal email to a friend? This will help choose words that sound right for the person/audience.
- Remember, good writing is always redrafted several times so when you are developing skills be prepared to rewrite your composition until you have a piece you are proud of.
- Try spending about 20–25 minutes writing each composition. Check it for mistakes at the end and correct them.
- Study well-written compositions by others and discuss the elements that make the composition suitable and interesting to read.

Timing strategies

As you get closer to completing your course, the amount of time you spend on the summary and note-taking exercises will become more important.

- Remember to divide your time sensibly among all the questions you are presented with on any given paper. It's a bad idea to spend too long on any particular question and then not have enough time to complete all the questions.
- A good tip is to write down how long it takes you to produce a summary or note-taking exercise and then try to improve that time as you progress through your course.
- Remember, though, that the time has to include all the stages of the exercise, such as reading the question carefully, final checking and making last-minute improvements. These are very important and can make a big difference.

Finally, if you persevere with the task until you are satisfied with the result, I can guarantee your skills will steadily improve. Think of yourself as a surgeon who cannot leave an operation half-done! Take care to complete the task well, and each time your work will improve a little more until you are doing good work with more and more enjoyment. Good luck and enjoy the eventual success you deserve.

Marian Barry, 2018

Science and the body
Note-taking 1

Read the article about special hi-tech spectacles that are being adapted to help children suffering from dyslexia. Then write short notes under each heading.

Tackling dyslexia in children

Children who are dyslexic have problems processing specific visual information, resulting in trouble reading and also difficulty with writing. Until recently, it was thought to be language-related areas of the brain which were deficient, but new research suggests that dyslexics have difficulty with the control of eye movement, or 'eye wobble'.

Scientists based at the QinetiQ Laboratory and researchers at the Dyslexia Research Trust are working together to adapt special glasses known as hi-tech specs (spectacles) to help dyslexics. These specs, originally developed to monitor the eye movements of fighter pilots, are being adapted into small versions for children as young as five.

It is hoped the technology will help children like the six-year-old boy who said to Dr Sue Fowler, a researcher at the Dyslexia Research Trust's clinic, 'Do you want to know a secret? All the words on the page move and I don't know how they do it because they don't have any legs.' Other children with dyslexia may report a disturbing sensation of 'glare' from the printed page, making them rub their eyes frequently. In some dyslexic children, reading causes a headache.

Professor John Stein, professor of neurology at Magdalen College, Oxford, has spent 20 years researching the connection between lack of eye control and reading difficulties. He says, 'We are visual people and eye movements are possibly the most important movements we make because they allow us to inspect the world around us. I believe problems with eye wobble account for up to two-thirds of dyslexia cases.'

'Dyslexia is not a disease. It is a brain difference, like left-handedness. We also believe that a cell in the brain, the magnocell, is related to eye movement. It seems that magnocells in dyslexics do not develop as well as those in good readers.'

The professor, who trained at Oxford and St Thomas's Hospital in London, will be meeting government officials to prepare for a trial of the hi-tech specs in primary schools in London and Hampshire. Professor Stein and his colleague Dr Fowler used the first prototype on a child last summer.

Professor Stein explains, 'Eye wobble is not obvious to the naked eye. The movements are small and very rapid. The hi-tech specs, which are worn for only a few minutes during tests, are the most accurate technique we have for detecting the amount of eye wobble. The child focuses on a point 45 centimetres away and then follows a moving target. The specs show whether the child's eyes are tracking steadily, or whether they wobble. We would like the specs to be mass-produced, becoming cheap enough to be used in all primary schools.'

Dr Fowler adds, 'We see 800 children a year from all over the country. They are mostly aged seven to twelve, but people of any age can be assessed. Because we are a charity and investigations are part of our research, children are seen free.'

'Children's brains are flexible enough to enable them to improve their eye control so it's important to identify young dyslexics early. After seeing them at the clinic, we give patients daily exercises to enable them to keep their eyes still and fixed on one object. In time, we believe these exercises become marked onto the brain. The result is that reading improves greatly.'

Problems a dyslexic child may complain of

- ....
- ....
- ....
- ....
- ....

Original use of the hi-tech specs

- ....

How the specs are used to test children for dyslexia

- ....
- ....
- ....

Treatment after the tests

- ....

Skills builder

Using the ideas in your notes, write a paragraph on the ways dyslexia may affect children, a technique for diagnosing dyslexia and how dyslexia can be treated. Write about 100 words (and not more than 120 words). Use your own words as far as possible.

TIP — **Being aware of your reading speed**

The speed at which students feel comfortable reading is a very personal matter and there is no doubt that individual speeds of reading vary a lot. Reading speed does not show how intelligent someone is, although young people often believe it does.

The fact is we all speed up and slow down as we read, depending on the difficulty of the content. We often do this without thinking, whether we are reading for pleasure or reading for information. We sometimes read groups of words quite fast, understanding the information quickly and easily, without any conscious effort. You may be surprised by how quickly you 'get through' several chapters of an exciting novel. On the other hand, we naturally slow down or reread a section of text when we want to be sure that we are getting the correct meaning from what we are reading.

Next time you read, you could try to be more aware of your reading speeds. When practising exam-style exercises, slow down a little if you begin to feel confused. Reread a sentence or group of words, checking back with the question to see if this bit of text contains relevant information. Approaching your reading in this way is a more mature attitude to study than rushing through without understanding. Don't be worried about taking more time, as the few extra seconds of double-checking are definitely worth it.

Summary 1

Read the internet article about the role of the placebo in medicine. Write a summary outlining what a placebo is, and the factors that increase the effectiveness of a placebo. Write about 100 words (and not more than 120 words). Use your own words as far as possible.

All in the mind?

Before the 20th century, doctors discovered that inert substances, with no active chemical ingredients, could have a dramatic effect on a patient's condition when other medicines failed to cure them. Doctors used these fake or pretend medicines in the hope that they might stimulate a patient's personal healing powers. They found that a person's belief in the power of the treatment was enough by itself to make them better. Patients might be prescribed fake medicines by doctors when other treatments had failed. Medicines of this kind became known as placebos, from the Latin 'to please'. It seems that placebos can affect the brain in some way, resulting in positive changes.

In modern times, clinical trials (research studies to investigate the best medical approaches to help patients) have demonstrated that placebos can be very effective for about 30 per cent of people. Placebos are considered especially valuable for subjective health conditions that have a psychological component, such as anxiety, pain or sleep disorders.

Maya dos Santos, a hairdresser, recently took part in a clinical trial to find out whether a placebo could help her lose weight. Maya says she had no idea that the slimming pills she was prescribed on the trial were a placebo. 'I was delighted when I was asked to participate as I wanted to lose weight to look good at my son's wedding. My previous attempts to slim had failed and nothing seemed to work. I believed in the pills and that made a difference. While I was on the trial, the doctor's advice was to take more exercise and to eat in moderation. To my amazement, I had no hunger pangs or cravings. I used to be obsessed with fatty food and high-calorie treats. I was convinced it was the slimming pills which decreased my appetite and took away my desire to snack. Instead, I enjoyed nutritious meals.'

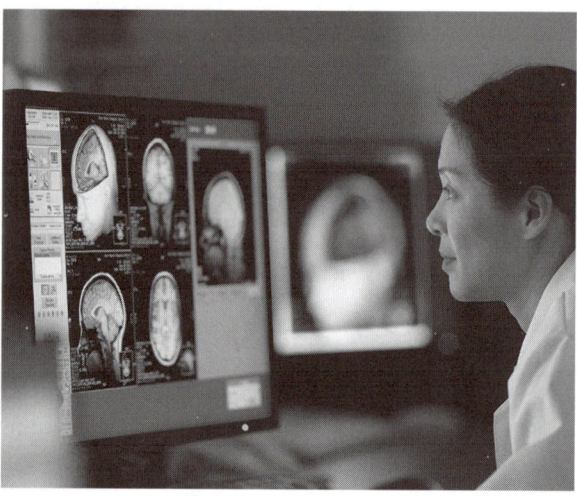

Soon Maya was receiving compliments about her trim shape, glowing skin and glossy hair. She says, 'It was thrilling when the doctor confirmed that I had reached my target weight. I had never felt more energetic and had a new zest for life. My only regret was that the pills had not been available before. I was stunned when he explained that the tablets were a placebo and contained nothing but a bit of flour and water.'

Maya clearly had a strong belief in the power of the pills and Professor Miller, who organised the project, says that this is important. 'We do not fully understand how a placebo works because the mind is so complex. However, the size and colour of the pills seem to matter. Large red or blue pills are perceived as more powerful than small white pills. Injections create even stronger expectations of a successful outcome. Giving strict instructions to follow also helps.'

Maya says, 'I was given big blue tablets to take 15 minutes before meals and I was careful to check the time was correct.' She adds, 'Halfway through the trial, I received an injection. I believed it boosted weight loss but I now know the nurse was injecting water.'

In addition to the pills, Maya was supported by a nurse. She says, 'Justina rang me on my mobile regularly and was so sympathetic. She praised me for my efforts.' Professor Miller says that comfort and reassurance help perhaps because they generate feel-good hormones.

The professor insists that the imagination also plays a powerful role. During the trial, Maya used her imagination to visualise the pills burning fat. Maya smiles as she explains, 'I pictured myself slim and radiantly healthy, wearing stylish clothes.'

It is unethical to prescribe a placebo without the patient's consent, unless they have agreed to be part of a clinical trial. Does Maya feel cheated? 'No!' Maya declares. 'It was not unfair. My mind is powerful — that is something I did not appreciate enough. Positive thinking helps me achieve my goals. My self-respect and self-esteem are higher now. What's more, I have just bought a gorgeous new trouser suit for the wedding!'

> **TIP** Ethical issues
>
> This article raises an ethical issue – the use of placebos. It is an ethical issue because some people might think it is harmful to prescribe placebos to sick people who believe they are being given genuine medicine.
>
> An ethical issue raises 'moral and ethical concerns' – involving questions of right and wrong.
>
> However, the tone used to describe the placebo response is not sensational. Ethical issues are not necessarily discussed in an emotive way. The article distinguishes clearly between medical theories expressed by the professor and the emotional and psychological reactions of the patient. Some of the professor's phrases sound cautious, for example: *we do not fully understand; perhaps because it may*. The idea of the article is not to give false hope that the placebo is a 'miracle cure'. The writer's aim is to interest readers who have no specialist knowledge and encourage them to make up their own minds.
>
> The task focuses on finding the facts and evidence about the placebo response. This is shown by the key words for the answer: **what** a placebo is, **why** it may help and the **factors** that can make it more effective. These key words are clues that help you understand the idea of a placebo and the potential seriousness of its use.

Note-taking 2

Read the article about the increase in the resistance to antibiotics. Then write short notes under each heading.

Antibiotic resistance

For many years, doctors have prescribed antibiotic medicines to help their patients recover from a wide range of common illnesses including nose, ear and throat problems, chest infections and stomach upsets. Antibiotics are also given for many more serious infectious diseases. In hospital, antibiotics have been relied on to help patients get over the health problems that can occur following surgical operations.

Unfortunately, some antibiotics now seem to be less powerful at overcoming serious bacterial infections. Scientists and doctors believe that there is growing evidence that antibiotics are no longer dependable. In hospitals, for instance, there have been many cases of patients who have developed a resistance to antibiotics. As a result, doctors and nurses are finding these patients much more difficult to treat. For example, tuberculosis (TB) used to be curable with antibiotics but now about 6 per cent of strains of six TB do not respond to a variety of antibiotics. Some new kinds of antibiotic-resistant infections are called superbugs. The superbug 'MRSA', for example, which patients might catch during a stay in hospitals, cannot be cured by antibiotics.

Scientists have always known that bacteria will eventually develop resistance to antibiotics. It was simply a matter of time. However, in recent times, this natural process has speeded up. Dr Afzaz, a surgeon who works in infection control in Brazil, believes we need to stop antibiotic resistance from accelerating. He thinks that part of the problem is that patients are not taking antibiotics in the correct way. He tells his patients that they should always complete the course of treatment he prescribes for them. However, he knows that some people stop as soon as they feel better, which can trigger resistance. Another issue is that patients sometimes share their medicine with family or friends for whom it was not prescribed. In addition, Dr Afzaz believes that some doctors prescribe antibiotics for illnesses such as colds, flu or other common viruses, which do not respond to antibiotics.

Dr Afzaz says, 'If people are suffering, they should rest, but some of my patients don't want to take time off work to get better. They ask me to prescribe antibiotics because they believe these are the most effective drugs. Also, when parents have sick children who have caught a cough or a cold, they automatically think the best

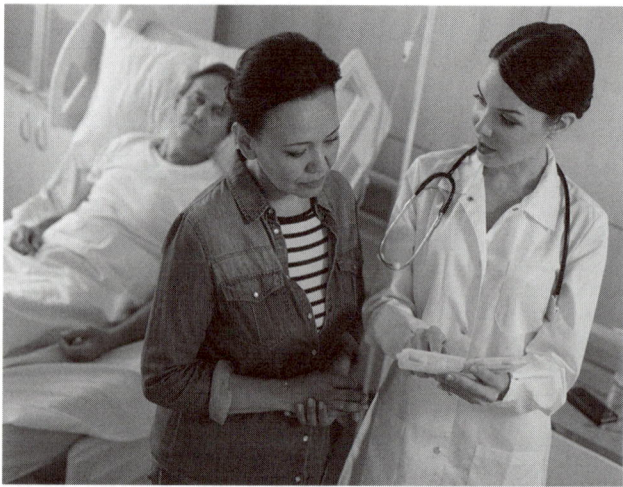

medicine is antibiotics. However, taking antibiotics, whether in liquid or tablet form, will not help you can recover any more quickly if the illness you suffer from is a virus.'

The World Health Organization (WHO) has given warnings that we are moving towards a 'post-antibiotic era'. In future, antibiotic resistance may result in more complex treatment for bacterial infections. Medical staff may no longer be able to use one course of medication to cure a single illness. Patients suffering from a bacterial infection may have to undergo multiple treatments over a longer time period and this will be more costly. Those on low incomes may not be able to afford to pay for all the prescriptions, so they are less likely to complete their treatment or may simply not go to the doctor when they are unwell because they are worried about the cost. WHO says that we will see a rise in infection-related deaths in future, especially in the world's poorest countries.

Pharmaceutical companies are hoping to develop a new class of antibiotic but have not yet succeeded. In the meantime, Dr Afzaz thinks we should pay attention to our general health. He says, 'A healthy lifestyle based on nutritious food and exercise will strengthen the immune system, making us more able to fight off disease without any medication.'

Reasons for rise in antibiotic resistance

- ....
- ....

Consequences of resistance

- ....
- ....
- ....
- ....
- ....
- ....

Scientific research focus

- ....

Skills builder

Using the ideas in your notes, write a paragraph explaining the effects of antibiotic resistance. Write about 100 words (and not more than 120 words). Use your own words as far as possible.

> **TIP** **Using linking words**
>
> When writing a summary, you often have to make a series of separate points. You can link them in different ways.
>
> To build up a list of points, use **linking words** such as *firstly, secondly, also, in addition, as well as, furthermore* and *moreover*.
>
> Linking words that show **contrast** include *but, although, on the other hand, in spite of, despite, however* and *nevertheless*.
>
> Words for **reasoning** include *because, as, since* and *for this reason*. Result or consequence can be expressed by *so, consequently, therefore* and *as a result*.
>
> You can **round** up your argument or list of points with expressions such as *finally, on balance, to sum up* and *in conclusion*.
>
> Apart from showing that you can reason and sequence your ideas clearly and logically, using linking words will also demonstrate that you are in control of sentence structure, and your paragraph will flow much better. This will help you to improve the quality of your answer.
>
> Reflecting on your learning also helps you become more objective about your progress. You will think more clearly about how your skills are improving and the ways in which you want to develop them further.

Summary 2

Read the article about allergies and then write a summary outlining why people may develop allergies and how modern medical techniques can help. Write about 100 words (and not more than 120 words). Use your own words as far as possible.

The enemy within

Allergy has become more and more common over the last 30 years. Now one-third of us are affected by allergy at some point in our lives and half of these sufferers are children. In the UK, three million people suffer from asthma, and five per cent of children suffer from food allergy.

Allergy is a reaction that occurs when the immune system has a strange and unnecessary reaction to a substance that is normally harmless, such as pollen or peanuts. The immune system is there to protect the body against outside attackers, including viruses, bacteria and parasites. To defend your body against an attacker, the immune system remembers these dangerous micro-organisms and attacks them if it meets them again. This work is done by antibodies. The immune system in allergy sufferers makes antibodies against harmless substances because it mistakenly believes them to be dangerous.

An allergic reaction may not happen the first time a sufferer meets an allergen (the substance causing the reaction, such as pollen, milk or strawberries). Sometimes people can eat nuts for years and then suddenly become allergic to them. What has happened is that the immune system has now decided the substance is dangerous and has made an allergy antibody. This antibody then attaches itself to cells that contain histamine. When the antibodies meet the allergen the next time, they attempt to destroy it. As they do that, the surface of the cells is broken and histamine is released. The histamine and other chemicals inflame the tissues. This leads to the symptoms of allergy, such as swelling, rashes, sneezing, sore eyes and breathlessness. Anaphylaxis is the most severe allergic reaction of all and is most often triggered by wasp or bee stings or peanuts. This must be treated immediately.

Allergies run in families. Some people are born with the ability to make lots of allergy antibodies, and they are more likely to develop allergies and allergic disorders such as hay fever and asthma.

Experts believe more people have developed allergies because of changes in our lifestyle that have exposed us to more allergens. We eat more processed foods, with a wide range of additives and colourings. More and more people in countries with cold climates have central heating and double-glazing, making houses warmer and less draughty – an ideal environment to breed the house dust mite, which some people are allergic to.

There may also be a link between allergies and antibiotics. At one time our immune systems were kept busy fighting off disease and trying to win the battle for health, but antibiotics have reduced the amount of work our immune systems have to do. Now experts think they may direct spare energy to harmless substances such as strawberries. In other words, our immune systems have become oversensitive.

A good deal of research is being devoted to finding a cure for allergies. Sufferers may be given medicine to control symptoms, and they may also be offered tests to find out which substances trigger allergic reactions so that they can avoid contact with these in future.

| TIP | Writing concisely |

The summary question asks you to write 'about 100 words' – you are allowed to write a few words under or over 100, but not more than 120 words. When practising summary writing, however, think about ways you can save on the number of words you use.

For example, **do not copy** out whole sentences from the text as this usually leads to using too many words. Also, try to use one collective noun instead of several separate nouns from the text. The **collective noun** you need may actually be in the text – for example, *allergen* can be used to refer to a list of substances such as *pollen*, *milk*, *strawberries*, *nuts* and so on. You have to decide yourself whether it is necessary to name each item separately in your summary or whether it is possible to use the collective noun. As well as reducing the number of words you write, using collective nouns shows that you have a good command of English.

Animal life
Note-taking 3

You are going to give a talk to a group of school friends hoping to take part in a whale-watching activity holiday, observing whales, porpoises and dolphins. Using information from the internet article, write short notes under each heading, as a basis for your talk.

The thrill of watching whales

When I volunteered to spend a summer on a land-based whale-watching project in the west of Scotland, the project secretary warned me, 'You have to be able to detect the whales from the shore – it's not as easy as you think.' Although I assumed I was well qualified for the job, at the start of the project I often imagined I could see dorsal fins in the dark tip of every wave and dolphins leaping in the wake-tracks on the water made by passing boats. I had a few embarrassing moments, screaming 'Whale!' before realising that what I was pointing out were only waves breaking over submerged rocks, not sea creatures at all!

After a while, I trained my eyes to 'see' – to distinguish between waves splashing over rocks and the rolling movement of whales underwater. I spent a lot of time just watching the sea through my binoculars, looking actively for anything that indicated sea life below. Learning more about the marine environment increased my ability to differentiate, especially in regard to the tides and currents, as these draw whales to certain areas. My binoculars enabled me to spot the fins of a porpoise against the darkness of the sea, and without a good pair of binoculars I definitely would have missed out on lots of stunning marine life.

In addition, I eventually realised that the birds provide us with signals that cetaceans – whales, dolphins and porpoises – may be in the area. Where there is a flock of feeding seabirds such as seagulls or gannets, there is often a whale feeding beneath them. Gannets are really easy to spot from a distance – they drop out of the sky at speeds of up to 100 kilometres per hour, spearing the surface and sending bursts of water up behind them. I also learned how to take my time, to be patient, peaceful and quiet so that the whales were undisturbed by my presence. One of my favourite moments occurred when I was sitting quietly by the sea on the Isle of Mull and a group of porpoises came in so close to the shoreline I could hear the gentle puffs of their breath.

If you want to try this activity, it is worth organising and planning carefully for whale-watching. I recommend having a notebook and pencil nearby to record details of what you've seen and the environmental conditions at the time. This is not only a helpful aid in general, but you can also contribute your sightings to research projects, such as the Sea Watch Foundation, that are monitoring the distribution of whales and dolphins.

Despite the early disappointments I had, I think there is undoubtedly something very special about watching whales. Nothing can compare with the secret thrill and the tranquillity of seeing a wild animal just doing its own thing.

How to get the most out of watching whales, porpoises and dolphins

- ....
- ....
- ....
- ....
- ....
- ....
- ....

Useful equipment for this activity

- ....
- ....

Skills builder

Using the ideas in your notes, write a paragraph explaining how whale watching can be made as satisfying as possible. Write about 100 words (and not more than 120 words). Use your own words as far as possible.

> **TIP** Selecting relevant information
>
> Often no word limit is given in the instructions for the note-taking exercise, and so students sometimes copy out long extracts from the text, hoping to 'cover' the required information for the answer in this way. This strategy does not produce good notes because you have to show that you have the skill of extracting only the relevant information. **Select information carefully**. If you copy out a large amount from the text, you will not be rewarded for it, even if what you copy contains some of the relevant points.
>
> Your notes should be **clear and concise**, and you do not need to write complete sentences. You should find one piece of information for each bullet point given.
>
> Don't worry if you can't find information to answer the question at the beginning of the text. The question may be designed to require information that comes later in the text.

Summary 3

Read the article about zoo cats. Write a summary outlining the signs of stress that big cats in zoos may show and what could be done to make them feel more comfortable in a zoo environment. Write about 100 words (and not more than 120 words). Use your own words as far as possible.

Why zoo cats lose their cool

Lions and tigers are stars of the show at most zoos. But the stress of celebrity status can cause them and other big cats on display to behave abnormally.

Researchers in the USA have found that big cats living near visitor areas are more likely to be disturbed in their behaviour. For example, during the day they may pace aimlessly back and forth. They also spend an unusual amount of time cleaning themselves, licking themselves and generally grooming. They are also noticeably more vigilant and keep a careful watch at all times. They prick up their ears and move around as though they feel the need to be on guard against threat. This is all strange and abnormal behaviour for nocturnal felines, who are normally only active at night. They should not be at all suspicious during daytime. In fact, big cats are usually asleep or resting during the day and only watchful at night.

The findings highlight the dilemma that zoos face when the welfare and happiness of the animals they look after cause conflict with the paying public's desire to get a close-up view of a lioness yawning or feeding her cubs. It seems as though disturbed behaviour in animals may well continue unless positive action is taken to improve the environment in which zoos house big cats and their smaller cousins in the cat family, such as caracals and bobcats. While a lot of work has gone into designing accommodation for monkeys, gorillas or chimpanzees, and studying how visitors affect the health of these primates, cats have been largely ignored.

Jennifer Ryback of James Madison University in Harrisonburg, Virginia studied seven species of cat living at the National Zoological Park in Washington, DC. All the cats, including lions, tigers, caracals and fishing cats, showed abnormal behaviour, and Ryback found that those housed near the public spent more time acting unnaturally than those that lived further away.

'Typically a cat will be resting during the day, which is certainly not what the public wants to see', says Ryback. When the cats seem distant or appear to be ignoring people, visitors actively try to attract their attention by waving or calling to them. They hope to get a reaction from the cats, such as hearing them roar or seeing them jump up a nearby tree. But the gesturing and shouting from observers make the animals even more stressed and irritated, putting them on the alert and making them pace around and groom more.

As well as improving the cats' enclosures by redesigning the space, including better use of ponds, bushes and trees, Ryback thinks zoos could enhance the quality of life for their cats. He suggests notices should be displayed telling visitors how to behave near the animals. In particular, people should show no excitement, not try to attract the animals or make a noise near them. Zoo attendants or keepers should also watch out for visitors behaving inappropriately near the animals and stop them. Ryback also suspects that keeping visitors just a little further away from the animals could make a big difference to the cats with no effect on people's enjoyment.

> **TIP** Punctuation
>
> Correct punctuation makes a difference to the clarity of your work. It is very important to use basic punctuation such as full stops and capital letters accurately.
>
> A **full stop** is used to show the end of a complete sentence. Try to get into the habit of putting in the full stops as you go along, by 'hearing' what you are writing in your head. Don't leave it until the end of your writing and then put them in – you are much more likely to put the full stops in the wrong place if you do this.
>
> Remember to use **capital letters** for the following: the first letter in a sentence, people's names and titles, nationalities, names of places, days of the week, names of months, book and film titles, and the pronoun 'I'.
>
> Try noticing how punctuation is used when you read English books and newspapers. This is an easy way to reinforce your understanding of how punctuation makes meaning clear.

Note-taking 4

Read the article about a science project to help polar bears in the Arctic. Then write short notes under each heading.

The secret world of polar bears

It is a bitterly cold winter's day in the Arctic and a hungry polar bear is searching for food. He stops by a waterhole hoping to catch a seal. When a seal emerges from the water, the polar bear grabs it. After feasting on the seal's blubber, the thick layer of fat under the seal's skin, the polar bear wipes his mouth on fresh snow before walking away, leaving big paw prints as he goes.

Teams of scientists and conservation workers are currently conducting studies on polar bears such as this one in the Arctic. They can be very hard for scientists to spot because their fur blends in so well with the snowy landscape, but even more so because female polar bears and cubs often hide themselves away in underground dens.

So how do scientists gather their research if it is so rare to encounter the bears? The answer is, astonishingly, in the paw prints that the bears leave behind in the ice. Skin cells are contained within these snowy prints, and so by collecting samples of the prints the bears leave behind, scientists can send these off to laboratories to test for DNA. DNA is a genetic code which carries hereditary information passed from parents to their young. The results from these DNA tests can help scientists to identify the unique characteristics of an individual polar bear, such as its eye colour, sex and size. Samples from paw prints allow scientists to learn a great deal about the number of polar bears in existence; it provides a reliable way to tell one polar bear from another and therefore analyse whether the polar bear population is steady or in decline; a very important factor in helping to look after the species.

Finding dens

Several kilometres away from the waterhole, a polar bear sleeps peacefully inside her underground shelter, or den. At about a metre deep, the den is invisible from the outside and the entrance is blocked by snow to keep the den warm. Safe and secure, this polar bear is waiting to give birth in a few weeks' time. How do scientists know she is here? Biologists have developed a novel method of finding polar bear dens and filming inside them. Aeroplanes fly over the Arctic landscape using specially adapted cameras which record the ground temperature. If the camera detects a rise in temperature, it is likely that a polar bear den lies beneath the surface. This is because female polar bears produce heat, which is then transferred to their surroundings. Identifying polar bear dens is a vital part of the research programme – when a polar bear gives birth to her cubs, they will remain in the den until they are three months old and strong enough to survive their cold, Arctic habitat. Knowing the location of these dens means that biologists can help to protect the polar bear families that dwell in them by making sure they are not accidentally driven over or disturbed by human activity.

Scientists are continuing to learn more using new kinds of technology. It is thought that drones (remotely operated aircraft) might be used more often in the future.

Uses of the paw print samples

- ....
- ....
- ....
- ....

Features of the den

- ....
- ....
- ....
- ....
- ....

Examples of the ways polar bears are protected

- ....
- ....

Skills builder

Using the ideas in your notes, write a paragraph outlining what scientists are doing in the Arctic and how their research has helped to protect polar bears. Write about 100 words (and not more than 120 words). Use your own words as far as possible.

> **TIP** **Predicting the content of a text**
>
> Look carefully at any headings, subheadings, pictures or charts to get a general idea of what the text is about before you start to read. Think carefully about the purpose of the text and the writer's intended audience. Is it designed to give the reader help and advice, or information and explanation? When you have recognised who the writer is writing for and why, you will be more able to predict the possible content. You will also be more receptive and alert to the type of vocabulary used, and this will help you to understand the text better. For example, in this text about the scientific study of polar bears in the Arctic you can expect to find vocabulary specifically relating to science, polar bears and their environment, including: *paw print, fur, ice, snow, den, cubs, biologists, DNA, samples, analyse, results.*

Summary 4

Read the internet article about the declining number of ocelots (wild cats) in Texas. Write a summary explaining why the ocelot population in Texas has gone down and what has been done to stop this trend. Write about 100 words (and not more than 120 words). Use your own words as far as possible.

Undercover cats

Ocelots are widespread in Mexico, South America and Central America. A small number also live in Texas, in the USA. These wild cats, which are about twice the size of domestic cats, were once hunted for their beautiful spotted coats. Now different dangers threaten them, especially the fifty or so that live in Texas.

All ocelots need a dense habitat to hide in, whether it is forest, mangrove or thick grass. In Texas, this coverage is provided by thick scrubland. Scrubland is an area of bushes growing 2–3 metres high, so thick you can only see about 1.5 metres inside it. To get inside, a child would have to crouch down low and crawl in on their hands and knees. Sadly, not much of this particularly thick scrubland is left in Texas. Much of the ocelots' habitat has been destroyed by landowners who have used it to build new homes for people. As well as housing developments, the habitat has also been lost because farmers and agricultural organisations have started grazing cattle or growing crops in former scrubland areas.

However, the reduction in the extent of the scrubland isn't the only problem. In Texas, there are only two small populations of ocelots still in existence. Each group lives in a different area of scrubland. The areas are separated by open fields 30 kilometres apart. The wild cats are shy and refuse to leave their bushy cover to risk crossing the open fields that separate one group of ocelots from the other group.

You might think that by staying in separate groups, under the cover of their scrubland environment, ocelots would be safe and flourish, but unfortunately this behaviour is leading to the opposite result. The two groups of ocelots no longer mix and, as a consequence of being confined to one group, they have begun mating with close relatives, which causes serious problems.

Jan Janecka is a scientist who studies ocelots. He explains that inbreeding reduces the rate of reproduction. As a result, ocelots have fewer kittens so the ocelot population is falling. He adds that even when kittens are born, they are weaker and some die at birth. Those that do survive are likely to die in their early years.

Concerned people have begun to take steps to help resolve this worrying situation. Landowners in Texas have decided to preserve the thick scrubland that ocelots prefer instead of letting it be used for commercial purposes. As well as keeping the scrubland, landowners are also starting to allow bushes to regrow on the wild land that connects the two areas where the ocelots live. This will encourage the ocelots to travel from one group to the other to find mates because they will feel protected by a safe corridor of scrubland.

Jan is concerned, however, that this approach will not work fast enough to save the ocelots in Texas from extinction. The kind of habitat that ocelots need takes decades to grow. 'We are running out of time. Ocelots are an endangered species in Texas. Without more help, these ocelots could be gone in 50–60 years' time', Jan says.

So, while they are waiting for the scrubland to finish growing, Jan and other dedicated scientists have resolved to mix the two groups in Texas. They plan to use drugs to tranquilise some of the ocelots and physically move them from one group to the other while they are asleep or drowsy. They would also like to introduce a few ocelots from Mexico into the Texan populations. A few years ago, when panthers living in the American state of Florida were having problems finding enough mates, scientists introduced panthers from Texas to the Florida population. 'The panthers made a comeback', Jan says. 'The panther population is fine now. It should work for ocelots too.'

Humans don't feel threatened by ocelots, so Jan is optimistic that the programme will be successful. 'Ocelots are small creatures. They are not dangerous, and don't attack people or cattle – though they have been known to steal a chicken or two!' he says.

Just a few years ago, conservationists thought there wasn't much hope for the survival of Texan ocelots but now, thanks to the efforts of scientists like Jan and some conservation-minded Texan landowners, these magnificent creatures may make a great comeback in the USA.

| TIP | Specialised and technical terms |

Sometimes a text will contain a specialised or technical term, such as *scrubland*, which a student could not be expected to know. If this is the case, the specialised term is explained within the text, as it is here (*an area of bushes growing 2–3 metres high*).

When you write a summary, you may need to include **either** the specialised term **or** the explanation of it. **Do not use both**. You should choose either one way or the other of referring to it. The specialised term itself is usually briefer than the definition, so using it in your summary will help you to write more concisely.

The world of plants
Note-taking 5

Read the article about the tea tree. Then write short notes under each heading.

A natural antiseptic

Charlotte Baxter investigates the new cure-all of our times

In pharmacies and health food shops all over the world you will see products containing tea tree oil. It is a wonderful antiseptic, good for acne, dry itchy skin, bruises and burns. As an antibacterial agent, it will aid the treatment of skin diseases such as dermatitis and fungal infections.

I had no idea where the oil came from and I imagined a fruit similar to an olive from which an oil would be extracted. So when I was invited to visit Birditt Farm, a tea tree plantation near the small town of Dimbulah, 7114 kilometres west of Cairns in Queensland, Australia, I was intrigued and interested.

The tea tree is a low, conifer-like bush with a papery bark, and its flowers consist of cream-coloured spikes. The oil is distilled from the needles.

The plants are grown from very tiny seeds, which take from five to seven days to germinate. At about 2.5 centimetres high, the tiny seedlings are transplanted into trays for the next stage of the growing process. The seedlings are kept first in an intensive greenhouse atmosphere and are then moved to cooler shade houses, rather like large open tents.

The permanent staff at Birditt Farm are a jolly bunch and more than willing to let visitors help with looking after the seedlings. I was involved with transplanting the tiny seedlings into larger containers. This method, known as pricking-out, needs a fair amount of dexterity, and I am afraid I damaged the first few plants I handled. However, I soon learned to handle them appropriately, using the minimum of pressure, and enjoyed chatting to the other workers about their families and lives in the area.

Tea tree oil production is extremely labour-intensive, since pricking-out and care during the growing stage, including weeding, have to be done by hand. At busy times casual labour – usually backpackers or students looking for temporary work during college vacations – is employed. The workers are very enthusiastic at first, but soon tire in the hot, often humid, atmosphere of the glasshouses and have to pace themselves to get through the work required.

Irrigation is by large watering machines. The watering process has to be monitored from time to time to ensure that the plants are receiving the right amount of water.

When the tea trees are strong bushy plants, 130–200 centimetres tall, they are cut down to within 30 centimetres of the ground and put into large bins ready for the steam distillation process.

The steam raises the temperature of the oil in the leaves, and the oil then evaporates into a water-cooled condenser. After the vapour has condensed, the resulting oil and water mixture is discharged into an oil separator. Here the oil floats on the water and is finally drawn off.

The precious oil is then put into sterile stainless steel or plastic-lined drums. It is stored in these drums after the process of extraction is complete, before being shipped to a distribution centre.

The global use of tea tree oil is increasing quickly – its healing properties are Australia's gift for a healthier world.

Where you can buy tea tree oil

- ....

Properties of tea tree oil

- ....

- ....

How the distillation process works

- ....

- ....

- ....

- ....

- ....

- ....

Skills builder

Using the ideas in your notes, write a paragraph describing the tea tree, the properties of its oil and what happens to the oil after it has been drawn off. Write about 100 words (and not more than 120 words). Use your own words as far as possible.

> **TIP** **Describing a process**
>
> When describing a process, take care that you have understood and covered **each stage** of the process. In the note-taking question, there will be one bullet point for each stage. Look out for words such as *first*, *then*, *next*, *after* and *finally*, as these can be helpful clues to the sequence of events in the process.
>
> Passive forms are common in descriptions of processes, and you may find them useful in your notes. Examples in the article are: *the oil and water mixture is discharged* and *the oil is drawn off*.
>
> Finally, read through your notes to make sure the points make sense and that they are in the correct order. Also check that they do not repeat each other.

Summary 5

Read the article about rose growing. Then write a summary outlining how roses were used in previous civilisations and why the rose is called the 'flower of life'. Write about 100 words (and not more than 120 words). Use your own words as far as possible.

The rose, queen of all flowers

The ancient Egyptians appear to be among the first early civilisations to learn how to grow roses. In 1888, at Hawara in the El Faiyum region of Egypt, two-thousand-year-old roses were found in ancient graves. The discovery suggested roses were an important part of the elaborate burial ceremony that took place when an important person died. The roses found in the tombs are thought by modern experts to be the oldest preserved flowers ever found in the entire world. They must have been cut and dried before opening so that they would remain undamaged. Over the centuries, the roses had shrunk and wrinkled into tight balls, but on careful examination it was discovered that the petals themselves were hardly damaged.

Egypt's expertise in the mass cultivation of roses in early times led to the flowers becoming an important export product. At its height, the Roman Empire imported enormous quantities of the blooms from Egypt. Wealthy Romans loved the beautiful colours, soft texture and fragrances of roses and they would scatter layers of rose petals across the floors of their main halls. At Roman weddings, the newly married couple were crowned with roses.

The Romans eventually attempted to cultivate their own roses and, after much trial and error, they mastered the art of mass cultivation. Egypt then decided to concentrate on growing grains such as wheat and barley instead of roses. Economic conditions meant that grain soon took over as the number one agricultural product of the Nile valley.

Roses were appreciated in other early civilisations too, including Greece and Persia. They are a decorative feature on coins, sculpture, vases and ornaments dating back thousands of years. There is also evidence that roses were highly valued in China. The Chinese believed that fluids extracted from roses could be used to help treat a wide range of illnesses from toothache and earache to skin and chest diseases. The healing properties of the flowers were recorded in detail in their manuscripts.

In the modern world, the rose has not lost its popularity as the 'queen of flowers' – the name given to it by the Greek poetess Sappho. A rose is a romantic gift, and to this day more roses are sold than any other flower. Modern techniques have enabled botanists to create ever more beautiful hybrids, combining selected features of parent plants. Transportation by air makes it possible to grow roses in countries with favourable climates and sell them within 24 hours in lucrative markets all over the world. Tonnes of roses are transported this way every week. Roses from Ecuador can be bought in Holland, even though that country itself has an enormous rose-growing business.

The rose has everything a plant can have: roots, stem, leaves, petals, thorns, colour and scent. The combination of beautiful flowers and sharp, prickly thorns is seen by some as symbolising the opposites of beauty and ugliness, happiness and pain, love and hatred. This rich symbolism makes the rose deserving of its other name: the flower of life.

> **TIP** Identifying key words
>
> Students are usually advised to underline the **key words** in an exam-style question but are sometimes unclear what a key word is. Key words carry **important information**. They include verbs such as *describe*, *explain*, *outline*, *compare* and *contrast*. These verbs indicate the kind of analysis of the text you have to do.
>
> The key verb is followed by other content words that carry meaning. In between the key words are less important grammar words such as prepositions and articles.
>
> In the question, the words *in previous civilisations* are crucial because they tell you that your summary should not include information about the use of roses today. Similarly, the words *how roses were used* show that you should **not** include the information about the growing of grain in the Nile valley (because it is not about roses), or the fact that the roses found in 1888 in the ancient graves were in good condition (because it is not about their use).

Note-taking 6

Read the internet article about the history of chocolate and complete the notes under the headings provided.

Sweet talk

The botanical name of the cocoa tree, from which chocolate is made, is *Theobroma cacao*. The first word is Greek for 'food of the gods'. Depending on who you believe, this seductive substance is an effective mood lifter and good for the heart, or the cause of spots, headaches, obesity and stressed-out nerves. But almost everyone believes it is one of the most irresistible foodstuffs ever produced.

Now, we learn that chocolate has been around for a lot longer than was previously thought. Traces of it have been found in pots discovered in Mayan graves in Mexico, some of which date back to 600 BCE, which pushes back the earliest chemical evidence of chocolate by more than 1000 years.

Chocolate is made from the seeds or 'beans' of the cocoa tree – the leathery cocoa pod contains up to 100 beans. Aztecs in Mexico and Mayans in Belize worshipped the tree and used its beans as a form of currency. They also had the idea of crushing the beans, boiling them in water, then adding spices and drinking the resulting hot, frothy liquid. In the 16th century, Spaniards who landed in Mexico wrote of how the Aztec emperor Montezuma drank chocolate 'from pure gold cups ... with great reverence'.

In 1519, the explorer Hernán Cortés sent three chests full of cocoa beans to the Emperor Charles V, complete with instructions on how to use them. Later, Sir Francis Drake brought a tonne of cocoa beans back to England. They were destined for the court of Queen Elizabeth I, but were mistaken for sheep droppings and thrown into Plymouth harbour.

Gradually, chocolate became a part of European life. Rich aristocrats and the privileged elite adopted the habit of drinking it during the day. It was not until sugar was added to the drink, however, and it was served in coffee houses, that chocolate was bought and enjoyed by the general public. Cocoa plantations were developed all over the world to meet the growing demand and, as the export of cocoa beans increased, chocolate became more easily available to ordinary people in Europe.

The conversion of chocolate from a drink to a food began in the 1700s when cocoa was added to cakes and ice cream. The first attempts at making solid chocolate came in the early 1800s when cocoa beans were ground into a powder, heated, sweetened and pressed into a mould. The resulting product resembled the chocolate truffles we eat today, but had a short shelf life.

It was a Dutch chemist and food scientist, Coenraad van Houten, who in 1828 perfected the extraction of cocoa butter from beans, which enabled the production of solid bars we would recognise as chocolate today.

In the 1880s, Rudolph Lindt of Switzerland started adding extra cocoa to make a product that melted at 36 °C. This is just a degree below the core temperature of the human body, so for the first time chocolate would melt in the mouth but not in the pocket on a warm day. Around the same time, Daniel Peter, a Swiss candy-maker, added condensed milk developed by Henri Nestlé to chocolate, making a sweeter and smoother variety of what is now one of the world's favourite foods.

Meaning of the Greek name given to the cocoa tree

• ....

Chocolate is produced from

• ....

Why the chocolate drink increased in popularity in Europe

• ....

• ....

• ....

Problem with the first solid chocolate ever made

• ....

Nineteenth-century developments in the production of better solid chocolate

• ....

• ....

• ....

Skills builder

Using the ideas in your notes, write a paragraph explaining why ordinary people began to enjoy chocolate drinks and describing the experiments that took place in the nineteenth century to improve solid chocolate. Write about 100 words (and not more than 120 words). Use your own words as far as possible.

> **TIP** Puns, idioms and colloquial expressions in titles
>
> You probably remember being told to look carefully at the heading or title of a text before beginning to read. This is good advice because the title usually contains important information. However, titles sometimes can be difficult to understand fully. This may be because of techniques the writer uses, especially when using devices that aim at a humorous effect, such as **puns** – using words or phrases with more than one meaning.
>
> The author of this article chooses the title 'Sweet talk' because it has **two meanings**. It can convey the idea that the article is about sweets or chocolate, but it is also a popular phrase meaning the affectionate language we use with close friends to flatter them and to get what we want.
>
> When you find a heading surprising or strange, consider whether there could be a **hidden meaning**. You can become more familiar with popular expressions including puns and idioms through listening to popular songs in English, watching films, using social media and reading widely.

Summary 6

Read the article about the mangoes in your trolley. Then write a summary about how parts of the mango tree can be used and the ways problems producing mangoes for the world's supermarkets can be solved. Write about 100 words (and not more than 120 words.) Use your own words as far as possible.

The mangoes in your trolley

Wild mangoes come from the foothills of the Himalayas. They are by far the most important fruit in India and have been cultivated there for 4000 years. The arrival of the mango tree in other parts of the world was probably due to the Portuguese who carried mangoes via Goa to Africa, from where they eventually reached the New World. Mango trees are now so well established in many tropical countries that it might appear that they have always been there.

Like many tropical trees, the mango tree is a multi-purpose commodity. Its wood is prepared for use in building and experts say such timber is particularly good for boat building. Mango leaves can be fed to cattle in moderation.

Most of the mango crop is consumed in the areas where it is grown, but in recent years mangoes have gained in popularity across the world as people in temperate climates become increasingly eager to savour the delights of the fresh fruit.

The global market for mangoes is potentially very financially lucrative and mango producers are keen to exploit the fruit's growing popularity. Modern shoppers appreciate the fruit's high nutritional value (the mango is a good source of vitamins A and C, protein, fructose and fibre), but also expect it to look and taste perfect. Unfortunately for producers, the seedlings of mangoes are extremely variable in quality and many have to be rejected as below the standard required for propagation. For mass cultivation, producers now select only the highest quality seedlings that have the best chance of developing into good quality fruit.

Although the mango tree has spread from its native Himalayan foothills to all of the tropics, delivering the fresh fruit to the world's supermarkets presents a challenge as it does not travel well. Producers transport the fruit by speedy but costly air freight for minimum delay rather than risk the cheaper but slower road or shipping routes which, although saving money, can result in damage to the fruit.

Mangoes are usually in storage for some time after their arrival at their destination. The fruit must be kept cold or the sweet, juicy flesh will soon become overripe and the mangoes will be unfit for sale. Fortunately, extremely effective refrigeration is now available and this is the best way of preventing the fruit from deteriorating before it reaches the supermarket shelves.

Many of the mangoes in our supermarkets come from plantations established in Kenya. These mangoes are sold in the shops at quite a high price relative to other fruit, but the cost reflects the expense of air transport and top-quality refrigeration. Fortunately for the producer, shoppers are prepared to pay extra to enjoy this most delicious of tropical fruit at its best.

> **TIP** Using your own words
>
> Remember that, although instructions in exam-style questions tell you to 'use your own words as far as possible', words of technical meaning such as *seedlings* and *propagation* can be taken directly from the text. Also, you are **not** expected to find substitutes for every word in the text, provided you can show you have a wide enough vocabulary to use your own **words quite often**.
>
> It is your overall control of language, and the way you reorganise and structure sentences that is important.

Personal challenges
Note-taking 7

Read the article about a teenage girl who survived for three days in the Australian rainforest. Then make short notes under each heading.

Lost on the mountain

19-year-old trainee beautician tells how she survived for three days in dense rainforest

After three days of searching for Louise Saunders on the slopes of Mount Tyson in tropical northern Queensland, most people's only hope was that she had fallen down and was lying injured in one of the mountain's rocky gullies. The last thing they were expecting was for her to walk out of the rainforest at a local rubbish dump. She was scratched, cut, bruised and hungry but otherwise unharmed after her frightening ordeal.

'It was an experience and an adventure, but I would never want to go through it again', said Louise from Kidderminster, England, who was spending time fruit-picking and travelling in Australia.

Part of her remarkable escape was due to the weather conditions. It was unusually warm and dry. Also, the many streams running down the sides of the 660m Mount Tyson allowed her to refill the two water bottles she had brought with her. 'I didn't really sleep', said Louise. 'It was just so cold at night.'

Louise appears to have crossed over the long north-south ridge of the mountain before following a gorge down the southern slopes of the mountain to the tea tree swamps surrounding the Cardwell Shire tip.

The greatest mystery was how anyone could be so hard to find on a mountain almost surrounded by roads and covering only a few square kilometres. Police say the thick vegetation near the streams may have hidden her from search parties and helicopters. More surprising is the failure to spot her when she deliberately stayed out in the open. 'I stayed in the same place the whole day', she said. 'I chose to climb to the top of a waterfall because it was really open. I thought if they were going to see me, they would notice me there.'

The workers who found her at Cardwell Shire dump said they were amazed and dumbfounded at her survival in the harsh rainforest. 'She was just yelling out when she saw us', said Louis Maund, who was on duty when Louise appeared outside the fence surrounding the dump.

Louise's mother told television reporters, 'Louise was so resourceful. I am so proud of her. She remained calm when a grown man would have been terrified.' This area of Queensland is known for its dangerous wildlife and the treacherous plants. The jungle is infested with taipan, one of the most poisonous snakes in the world. Less dangerous but irritating all the same is the wait-a-while vine. The vine's tendrils carry sharp hooks that lacerate bare skin.

The search parties moved through the forest in groups of four, armed with walkie-talkies and keeping close together in case of danger. 'You're clambering over these big boulders with loose rocks underfoot', said searcher Kieran Falnaga, 23, who admitted he was exhausted after a few hours of searching. George Guido, 28, another member of the search party, said, 'We were hacking through the undergrowth – we couldn't see more than two feet in front of us.'

Louise had been fruit-picking on local farms to finance her extended trip, and had already visited Perth, Darwin, Uluru and Alice Springs.

What helped Louise to survive

- ....
- ....

How Louise tried to attract attention

- ....
- ....

The special dangers to walkers exploring the area

- ....
- ....

How the search for Louise was organised

- ....
- ....
- ....

Skills builder

Using the ideas in your notes, write a paragraph outlining Louise's plans for visiting Australia, what helped her to survive on the mountain, and how she tried to attract the attention of people searching for her. Write about 100 words (and not more than 120 words). Use your own words as far as possible.

> **TIP** **Dealing with unknown words**
>
> Don't worry if you don't understand every word in a text. You can understand a text well without knowing every single word.
>
> In this text, perhaps you found the words *gullies* and *gorge* unfamiliar, for example. If you come across strange words such as these, try to **make a guess** at their meaning by studying the context. Here the word *gullies* is associated with places on the mountain where Louise might have fallen, so the situation being described might give you a good enough idea of what *gullies* might be.
>
> Also, even if there is some unusual or rare vocabulary in the text, you won't be expected to focus on this in your answer. The required answers are based on straightforward language that, as an IGCSE student, you could reasonably be expected to know. Difficult language from the text is avoided.

Summary 7

Read the article about students who spend a year abroad at a foreign university as part of their course. Write a summary explaining what students are expected to produce from a year abroad and how their home universities help prepare students for this experience. Write about 100 words (and not more than 120 words). Use your own words as far as possible.

Young ambassadors

Contrary to the beliefs of many of its opponents, going abroad to study at an overseas university whilst doing an undergraduate degree is definitely not an opportunity to be lazy. The year abroad in the host country provides students with a unique experience when they will live in a totally different community. Students have the chance to get insights into the history, culture and society of another country, as well as an opportunity to improve their academic skills. Besides attending lectures and doing coursework while abroad, students are required to complete a special cultural assignment for their home university.

The year overseas is also important to students on a personal level. It needs determination, perseverance, open-mindedness and a willingness to fit into a new life. The diversity of the experiences certainly broadens the minds of most undergraduates. Many language students now spend their year abroad in Spanish-speaking Latin America, French territories in the Caribbean or the Indian Ocean, or the Russian-speaking states that once formed part of the Soviet Union.

Home universities spend a great deal of time making sure their students have a realistic idea of what the year abroad will be like – they certainly do not simply wave goodbye to them for a year.

It is important, for example, that students do not expect the foreign university to be similar to their home university or indeed be like it in any way. In many universities, students attend talks and are given detailed information in checklists, guides, handbooks and web-based information. Students who went abroad the previous year and have now returned, answer questions on their experiences.

Although university staff make great efforts to reduce the culture shock some students feel on arrival in another country, the students have responsibilities too. When overseas, they have a duty to keep in close touch with their home universities, through answering regular questionnaires, for example.

Maintaining contact with their personal tutor at home via email, telephone or letter is essential. Tutors can only act quickly in giving support if they are kept informed by their students about their situation.

In my experience as a lecturer, returning students are usually brimming with exciting tales to tell of their experiences abroad. They return much more competent, with a more mature and thoughtful approach, and have acquired some valuable life skills.

> **TIP** Summarising more difficult texts
>
> Sometimes students say they find some texts harder than others. Perhaps this is because the information is more involved, the language level seems a bit higher, or the topic is unfamiliar. This article, for example, is about university students studying overseas so the topic may be outside your life experience but you can still consider it, especially since you may have a similar experience yourself in the future.
>
> If you find a text hard, **don't panic**. The most important thing is to make sure you have understood the question set, and then try to get a good general idea of the contents. Also, try to **be methodical** in your approach, take the material step by step and make sure that, in your answer, you have covered all aspects of the question.
>
> Even the more difficult-looking texts can be done very well when students follow the simple rules of not rushing, being careful about detail and making really sure that they have not missed out anything that is important for the answer. At the other extreme, students can lose marks because they rush through a text thinking it is 'easy', only to make silly mistakes because they do not take enough care and forget to follow the simple rules.

Note-taking 8

Your headteacher has asked you to give a talk to a group of school-leavers at a careers information evening. The topic of the talk is 'Taking a gap year'. (A 'gap year' is a year between leaving school and going to college or university.) Using information from the internet article, write a set of notes under the headings given, as a basis for your talk.

Taking a gap year

After exams, going to university or getting your first job isn't the only adventure to go for. Robert Bates said 'yes' to a year out in another country. Here he talks about his experiences.

I was pleased with my exam results, which secured me a place at university to study engineering. But I also wanted to travel before starting my course. I thought carefully about the kind of trip to do – just backpacking around the globe didn't appeal. Then a friend of mine told me about organisations that help students take a gap year.

Raleigh International, for instance, has projects all over the world for 18-to 25-year-olds. You can do so many different things, from gorilla-trekking in Uganda to rice-picking in China. I also heard about the Schools Exploring Society. It has three foreign expeditions a year, taking 16-to 20-year-olds on science and nature trips. I love being outdoors, and a mountaineering expedition to Alaska was on offer. I decided this was my chance to see the world and I signed up immediately.

There was one problem, though. To be allowed on the trip, I had to raise a large amount of money for my fare and expenses. It was daunting, but I thought about how to meet the target. To help me focus on getting temporary paid work, I posted my skills and personal qualities on my social media page. In the end, I washed cars, worked in a café and also sold off some of my old books, clothes and CDs. Actually, I only made the target six days before departure. Then, just before I was due to go, I started worrying. Can I do this? Am I fit enough? What if I see a bear?!

Seventy of us travelled to Alaska. The first two days after arrival were spent in a school hall preparing our equipment and five tonnes of food. Then, in groups of 12, we headed for the Talkeetna mountains. They were stunning. On the trip we dug paths, identified plant species and analysed soil acidity. It was tiring, but I kept thinking 'I can't believe I'm here.' Then we trekked over a glacier 1800 metres high. It was hard work and very cold, but incredible too.

After 13 years in the same school with the same friends, it was nerve-wracking but inspiring to be thousands of kilometres away, talking to people with different ideas on life. I learned a lot about tolerance – accepting other people for what they are. We had to help each other and it made me less selfish, as I had to consider other people before myself.

Looking back, a gap year was so right for me. I'm sure I would have burnt out in my first year of university if I'd gone straight from school with no break from studying. Instead of being distracted from my studies, my gap year has made me more able to concentrate and better at analysing information. Now, whenever I'm worried about anything, I think 'I did Alaska – I can do this!'

Organisations that offer gap year projects

- ....
- ....

Before trying to get work, it is useful to

- ....
- ....

How a gap year can develop your character

- ....
- ....
- ....
- ....

How a gap year can help you academically

- ....
- ....

Skills builder

Using the ideas in your notes, write a paragraph explaining what benefits you can get from a gap year. Write about 100 words (and not more than 120 words). Use your own words as far as possible.

> **TIP** **General notes from a personal text**
>
> Sometimes you might be faced with a text that tells a story from one person's point of view. In this text, for example, Robert explains what happened when he decided to take a gap year. The question asks you to present the information for a general audience, however, so you should use either the second person 'you' or a **neutral voice**. Do not use 'I' in your notes.
>
> Of course, notes don't have to be in full sentences, so it may not be necessary to use either pronoun. The main point to remember is that your notes have to be clear and make sense, so think carefully about the intended audience for them.

Summary 8

Read the article about a girl who lost her feet as a baby. Write a summary outlining how Vanessa has coped with the effects of her disability and Vanessa's reactions to her new legs. Write about 100 words (and not more than 120 words.) Use your own words as far as possible.

My daughter can achieve whatever she wants

Vanessa Hill lost her feet from illness at such a young age that she never knew what it was like to have them.

At 13 months old she was fitted with a set of prosthetic (artificial) limbs to assist her in learning to take her first baby steps. 'I should have been pleased, but the artificial legs were horrible', says Vanessa's mother, Jan. 'They weren't even the same colour as her skin and were cold to the touch.'

Problems began when Vanessa was older. 'I'd see people walking past me and they would stare and make comments. It upset me, and hurt Mum too, to see me so upset', says Vanessa. 'Mum told me to ignore what unkind people said and, in time, I was able to do that. When activities at school came up, like swimming and skiing, I was reluctant to take part but my mother encouraged me so much I decided to give the sports a go anyway, and now I enjoy them.'

'She was so brave and determined', says Jan. 'At first she took the teasing to heart and was very upset, but she just wouldn't give up. At home we gave her all the support we could and I think that made a big difference.'

A couple of years ago, the family saw a television programme about a girl in Cape Town, Laura Giddings, who had lost her leg in an explosion at a restaurant. Jan explains: 'Laura had been fitted with a silicone leg which was much more realistic-looking than the prosthetic limbs Vanessa had. I cried as I thought what a massive difference such natural-type legs could have on Vanessa's life. But with two other children to look after as well as Vanessa, there was no way we could afford to pay for silicone legs. We would have had to spend £5,500 on new legs for her every six months, as she is still growing.'

Not long afterwards, the school support worker rang the family and asked if there was anything she could do to help. 'I found myself spilling out everything about the private treatment', says Jan. A few weeks later the support worker called again to say she had come up with a plan to organise some fund-raising events to get Vanessa new legs. 'I was completely overwhelmed. The school organised raffles, cake sales and sponsored events. People we had never met sent donations. Every day we got cards from well-wishers, and the cheques just kept arriving.'

'When enough money had been raised, I contacted the orthopaedic centre and Vanessa was measured for her new legs. When the consultant showed us the sort of silicone legs Vanessa could have, we couldn't believe how realistic they looked. The specialists could match her exact skin tone.'

'I've got loads more confidence and love going shopping for shoes and clothes', says Vanessa. 'My legs look so real, and if you touch them they feel warm, like proper legs. But the best part is finally being able to do anything without having to worry about how my legs look. Now I'm just like everyone else.'

> **TIP** **Using appropriate tenses and correct names**
>
> Tenses are important in showing the time aspect of a story. In this story, for example, past tenses are used to show what happened before Vanessa got her new legs, whereas the present tense is used to describe her situation and feelings since she had new legs fitted.
>
> When you write your summary, be careful to use the **appropriate tenses** to talk about the past and the present. Study the words in the question carefully – these will give you ideas about the right tenses to use too.
>
> You should also be careful when several different people are referred to by name in a text. If you have to write about these people, be careful to use their correct names and try not to mix them up. If you do this, your writing will be clear and easy to understand.

Leisure and lifestyle
Note-taking 9

Read the article about the way people feel about the development of wind turbines close to their homes. Then make short notes under each of the bullet points given.

The ugly side of clean power

The noise, says Les Nichols, is a low thump-thump-thump that reverberates up to 22 times a minute. 'It's not there all the time, but you're always waiting for it', he says. 'It's a form of torture.'

Les lives besides a wind farm in Furness, a beautiful, scenic area in the north-west of England. For the past three-and-a-half years, he and his neighbours have had to put up with a level of noise that disrupts their sleep and causes constant stress. 'When the developers asked for permission for the seven giant turbines in this area, they guaranteed there would be no noise nuisance or disturbing sounds', he says. The wind farm is managed by Wind Prospect on behalf of its owner, PowerGen. Bruce Allen, a director of Wind Prospect, said that the fact that no action had been taken to close the wind farm suggested it had not broken planning rules. He added: 'The noise is a subjective thing – like living next to a busy road.' PowerGen says that it has installed special noise reduction software to eliminate the nuisance.

The government has plans to double the number of wind farms in an effort to get 20 per cent of electricity from renewable sources. Once regarded as unusual, wind farms are increasing in popularity as power companies take advantage of government subsidies and build turbines on windy sites.

Wind power also receives strong support from environmental groups such as Greenpeace and Friends of the Earth, which believe the problems of noise and ugly landscapes are less important than the reduced air pollution and lower carbon emissions we receive as a result of wind farms.

Residents, however, argue that having a series of giant wind turbines erected near their homes transforms a tranquil neighbourhood into an ugly industrial site. At the very least the farms – usually sited along the skyline to benefit from maximum wind – are a horrible eyesore.

Among the other unpleasant effects reported by residents' opposition groups are increased stress from noise vibration and many more visits to the doctor. Angela Kelly, who chairs the anti-wind farm residents' campaign group, Country Guardian, claims they make people ill.

Although wind farms are usually in rural areas of low population, there are no fixed rules about how near they can be to homes. Government advisers recommend they shouldn't be less than 1.5 kilometres from any house, but developers go as close as between 500 metres and 600 metres. Although Country Guardian have helped to stop the building of many turbines in the past decade, they say the pressure to build more turbines is steadily increasing.

Scotland, for example, has 120 potential wind power sites under consideration. A map produced by concerned residents shows that large areas of Scotland's horizon, coastline and countryside will never again escape the sight of the giant turbines.

Anti-wind farm pressure groups claim that the tiny amount of electricity they produce is not worth the environmental cost. And because the wind itself is unreliable, conventional power stations must be on standby in case they are needed.

The advantages of wind turbines, according to the government and environmental groups

- ....
- ....

Residents' views about the effects of turbines on the environment

- ....
- ....
- ....
- ....

Effects of turbines on residents' health

- ....
- ....

Why opposition groups think the turbines lack practical value

- ....
- ....
- ....

Skills builder

Using the ideas in your notes, write a paragraph on the benefits and drawbacks of wind turbines. Write about 100 words (and not more than 120 words). Use your own words as far as possible.

> **TIP** Generalising from factual information
>
> Factual items about the impact of modern technology on people's lives are quite popular topics. In this case, the wind-power technology is British-based, but the underlying ideas, including why the technology is developing and how it might affect people and the environment, are applicable to many different situations and parts of the world.
>
> It is useful when you are reading a text to think about the **ideas in general**, rather than only the particular situation described in the text. It is also helpful to think about how your own environment would be altered should these changes happen in your area, as this can help you to understand the implications.

Summary 9

Read the article about a boy who joined the circus. Write a summary outlining why Alex wanted to become a clown, and how his life has changed since he began training as a clown. Write about 100 words (and not more than 120 words). Use your own words as far as possible.

From schoolboy to clown

Alex Santas, 13, has always had a burning ambition to become a circus clown. A few years ago, his dream started to come true when, accompanied by his parents, he left home to begin training with the circus. 'When Alex was only three', says his mother Anna, 'we took him to the circus and he absolutely could not take his eyes off the clowns'. Alex still remembers that visit: 'I just loved the way the audience was looking and smiling at the clowns. If a juggler drops his clubs, or a trapeze artist falls, it messes up the act. But if a clown falls over, everyone thinks it's a great joke and roars with laughter.'

'Alex was so intrigued by the special power that the clowns seemed to have, he kept asking to visit the circus again', recalls his father David. 'At family parties he used to dress up as a clown and put on a performance doing juggling, comedy routines and magic tricks. Over the years, Alex's love of the circus began to affect the way Anna and I felt. His aspirations were rubbing off on us. Then, unexpectedly, I was made redundant from my job as a gas-heating designer. I was offered similar work with an agency, but Anna and I wanted to explore our dream, so we wrote away to the circus to see if there were any jobs.'

'Eventually David and I were offered jobs with the Moscow State Circus', explains Anna. 'It was so exciting. David worked as a spotlight operator and I worked in the box office, selling tickets. Most important of all, Alex had a chance to begin his training as a clown.'

However, Anna admits that there was a lot of difficult decision-making and soul-searching to do before they finally made up their minds. 'After all', she says, 'we were leaving our pleasant, centrally heated house with all its home comforts to live in a small caravan. But Alex was so thrilled at the prospect, and he seemed to have so much talent and flair, we thought, why not?'

After two years, the family joined Zippo's Circus. 'We now go touring, which is marvellous', smiles Anna, 'and David has been promoted to foyer operations manager'.

Although he is not old enough to perform in the circus yet, Alex is continuing to develop his clowning skills. 'I think this way of life is fantastic', he says. 'Since joining the circus, I have met people from all over the world. It's even better now that I'm allowed to go out with Dad to perform in front of school audiences when we're on tour.'

'People ask about my education', adds Alex, 'but wherever we are on tour, Mum organises a private tutor to come and teach me. I follow the same books as children at school and I've got a laptop. I just have to make sure I don't fall behind. I've got used to one-to-one teaching and really like it.'

And the future? 'I'm going to be a main clown in a circus one day', declares Alex firmly.

> **TIP** Developing imaginative skills
>
> This text focuses on a family's dreams and unusual lifestyle. Even if you have never been to a circus or thought about circuses before, try to use your imagination to put yourself into the situation, to understand what is special and appealing about it. Even though it may not appeal to you personally, ask yourself why someone might be attracted to the circus way of life.
>
> Developing your **imaginative skills** in this way will not only help you when reading about unfamiliar situations. It will also enable you to be more adaptable and to relate better to people in all aspects of your life.

Note-taking 10

Read the talk given by an expert about the Inca civilisation. Then write short notes under each heading.

The world of the Incas

Good afternoon, everyone. I am delighted to share my experiences as an archaeologist with you.

Ever since the age of 11, when I dug up a bronze statue in the garden and my parents found that it was 600 years old, I have been fascinated by the secrets of the past. My curiosity has taken me all over the world and I have just returned from an expedition to Peru. I have been working with an international team in the Andes Mountains excavating to uncover remains of an old Inca city, Machu Picchu.

The Incas were an American Indian people who arrived in the central Andes about 1250 CE. They built up an empire in South America that stretched across modern Peru and Ecuador to parts of Bolivia, Chile and Argentina.

The Incas were ruled by an emperor, who had absolute power. They developed a rich and complex civilisation, and had skills in engineering and architecture. They also studied astronomy – the movements of the planets. Ordinary people ate simple food – mainly vegetables, grains and dried fish. The capital was Cuzco. Like all Inca cities, it was beautiful, with paved roads and a magnificent palace. Quechua was the Inca language, but there was no system of writing. Although the empire was damaged by civil war and then conquered by the invading Spaniards in 1532 (who were attracted by Inca gold amongst other things), the Quechua language has survived. Thirteen per cent of the population of modern Peru speaks Quechua and it is also spoken elsewhere in the Andes.

When I was in Peru, I spent quite a bit of time working in the ruined city of Machu Picchu. You may have already heard of it because it is a World Heritage Site, and attracts tourists and experts from all over the world. It is a remarkable place and the remains of the city are fascinating.

Machu Pichu was built in a remarkable position. It was constructed between two mountain peaks high up in the Andes, about 2430 metres above sea level. It was a truly astonishing achievement to build the city in such a challenging mountainous location. It was made from stone cut without iron tools from a quarry on site. Wheeled vehicles were unknown, so hundreds of builders made the five-day walk from Cuzco to Machu Picchu.

Beautiful houses, stunning temples and even fountains were constructed. More than a hundred stone staircases were made to connect different levels in the city. Perhaps most impressive of all, an observatory was built so astronomers could watch the movements of the sun, moon and stars. What better place to do star-gazing than on a crystal-clear night high up in the mountains?

Archaeologists and historians have wondered why the city was built in such a remote and difficult position. One theory is that the site was chosen for religious reasons. The Incas believed that the gods they worshipped lived in the mountains and in water, so the landscape of Machu Picchu was perfect for honouring them.

The area was also a good place for the Incas to gather for religious observances, especially for the winter and summer solstices, the shortest and longest days of the year. A temple in Machu Picchu was designed at a particular angle so that when the sun shone through the window on the winter solstice it lit up a stone shrine.

An American explorer 'discovered' the site by accident in 1911 and Machu Picchu has fascinated us ever since. It is a mysterious place and perhaps one day more of its secrets will be revealed.

Achievements of the Inca civilisation, 1250–1532

- ....
- ....
- ....
- ....
- ....
- ....
- ....

Features of Machu Picchu

- ....
- ....
- ....
- ....
- ....
- ....

Spiritual practices

- ....
- ....

Skills builder

Using the ideas in your notes, write a paragraph outlining the importance of the Inca civilisation and why it ended. Write about 100 words (and not more than 120 words). Use your own words as far as possible.

> **TIP** **Practising with a friend**
>
> Have you thought about practising exam-style exercises with a friend? Studying with a friend who is also preparing for examination is more motivating than working alone and, because students sometimes put off studying, being together can help you to get down to the hard work of revising.
>
> If you are practising your note-taking and summarising skills, you can try the same exercise together. When you have finished, **check each other's work** and see what differences there are. Have either of you made any silly mistakes, such as copying words from the text incorrectly? You could also discuss whether you have found the relevant points from the text and consider what improvements could be made to each of your answers.

Summary 10

Read the article about Daphne and her experience of family meals. Then write a summary explaining the attitudes her family had to mealtimes when she was growing up and why mealtimes with her own children are usually tense. Write about 100 words (and not more than 120 words). Use your own words as far as possible.

What's for dinner, Mum?

I was born into a Latin family. That means I was raised in an environment in which food was a vital part of family life and family mealtimes were sacred. The scene around our kitchen table when I was a child must have seemed a bit like an advertisement for the perfect family. I remember us all sitting down to dinner every night, laughing and talking while we consumed huge platefuls of my mum's delicious home cooking.

Actually, when I was younger I sometimes thought my Spanish family was a bit too insistent about being at home for meals. When I was at college, for example, living miles from home, I used to have to go home every weekend for Sunday lunch. Although this wasn't always convenient, if I didn't turn up I ran the risk of my father cutting me off without my inheritance! Our lives were ruled by the idea that families who eat together, stay together and there were certain expectations regarding eating and mealtimes. In my family, no one ever ate in front of the TV or said, 'I'll grab a sandwich later.'

It's strange that, although I sometimes felt reluctant following these rules when I was a teenager, now, as a mother of two children myself, I've found that the old habits have come back. Now I insist that we all sit down together every evening and eat dinner – although frankly, I often wonder why I do this. I have to admit that our mealtimes are rarely civilised affairs, where people smile warmly, compliment the cook and enquire politely about each other's day.

Family meals in our house often start with a squabble between 11-year-old Frankie and 14-year-old Jessica about whose turn it is to lay the table, or why one of them has got a drink for themselves, but not for the other. Then, when dinner is served, the annoying grumbles about the food begin – of the 'I don't like soup / salad / anything healthy whatsoever' variety. 'Yuk!' said Frankie the other night as I put a dish of lovely home-cooked vegetables on the table.

Mealtimes also seem to lead to trivial quarrels about other things. Perhaps it's because we're tired and argumentative after a long day at work or school, but however much we try, my husband and I can't seem to avoid using this opportunity for telling the children off about the state of their bedrooms, their disregard for the value of money or their laziness. Other families, in my imagination, are spending mealtimes having intelligent discussions – about the state of the environment, perhaps.

Don't ask me why my family mealtimes are so challenging. Whatever the reason – too much eye contact perhaps? – I do know that I end up feeling disgruntled about the time I've spent preparing a tasty meal.

Maybe the kids are right after all, and it's time to hang up my apron, put away the saucepans and the cookery books, pick up the 'dial a pizza' menu and let it go.

> **TIP** **Becoming familiar with colloquial style**
>
> You may be faced with a chatty item like this article from a family magazine, so it is worth making yourself familiar with their style and approach. They tend to be more light-hearted and humorous, partly because there is often some exaggeration by the author to get a comic effect. The articles also tend to be targeted at a specific audience – in this case other mothers – so there are assumptions about shared experience. This experience may not necessarily reflect your own views or lifestyle, so you may need to think about the ideas carefully and discuss them with your friends.
>
> It is also useful, in general, to expand your knowledge of **colloquial language** such as let it go, **as** this will help you become more fluent in English and more able to use a variety of both formal and informal registers. If you take the time occasionally to read magazines in English or watch films, you will also extend your range of conversational English.

Trends – past, present and future
Note-taking 11

Read the internet article about how barcodes have changed supermarkets. Then write short notes under each heading.

Birth of a barcode

In 1948, Joseph Woodland, a young graduate student of engineering, relaxing on a beach in Florida, USA, observed the waves rolling back from the shore. He noticed the deep lines that the sea had made in the sand, and he was reminded of the way Morse code uses dots and dashes to convey messages. The thought came to him that black lines or stripes could be used to convey information on shop products in a code that a machine could read. However, computer technology was not advanced enough for his vision of a 'striped scan system' to be instantly workable.

As computers advanced and lasers were invented, the idea became more realistic. The striped scan system, or barcode, was gradually refined and improved over the years. In the 1950s, an engineer, David Collins, put black lines on railway carriages so they could be automatically read by a trackside scanner. The grocery industry of America also realised the potential of the innovation. If a laser scanner at the checkout could scan the product barcode, it could improve the grocery business for customers and retailers.

In 1969, members of the Grocery Manufacturers of America (GMA) met the members of the Association of Foodchains (AFC) to decide on a product code. The location of their conference was a hotel in Cincinnati, Ohio, USA. The GMA wanted an 11-digit code but the AFC argued for a simpler, seven-digit code.

The grocery businesses had many more meetings before they agreed on a barcode format. Finally, in 1974, at a supermarket in the town of Troy, Ohio, a 31-year-old checkout assistant named Sharon Buchan used a laser scanner to scan a packet of chewing gum. The details of the product and its price of 67 cents registered correctly. The invention of a barcode and laser scanner meant a new way of doing business in supermarkets had begun at last.

After 26 years, Joseph Woodland's barcode dream had finally come true.

Nevertheless, there were still obstacles to overcome. Retailers did not want to install scanners until food manufacturers had put barcodes on their products. Manufacturers were unwilling to put barcodes on their products until supermarkets had enough scanners. Eventually, large supermarkets realised that by using barcodes they could sell a wider range of products at lower prices so the high cost of the scanners could be balanced against increased sales. There was also better stock control as the scanner recorded all the details of the product, including the price and date of sale. Scanning products at the checkout could be done quickly so waiting time in queues was reduced, there was more variety of goods to choose from and customers were happier.

However, small family-run grocery stores struggled to keep up with the changes. The new system did not bring advantages to the owners of small shops. In fact, it was a barrier to success. Small stores did not usually have problems with customer service or management of their stock. The laser scanners were too expensive for their level of sales. Increasingly, the innovation meant smaller food shops lost custom and became less profitable. The trend moved in favour of larger supermarkets.

The barcode meant greater profits for big supermarkets and they expanded. They also sold new product lines, including non-food items such as saucepans, clothes and flowers. Eventually, the supermarket business became international as retailers found the barcode system enabled them to order and track products from all over the world.

History of the barcode

- ....
- ....
- ....
- ....

Benefits to large supermarkets

- ....
- ....
- ....
- ....
- ....
- ....

Skills builder

Using the ideas in your notes, write a paragraph outlining the ways developments in technology helped the barcode system to become possible and why small supermarkets did not benefit from the introduction of the barcode. Write about 100 words (and not more than 120 words). Use your own words as far as possible.

> **TIP** Developing a mature approach to study
>
> Students sometimes become very competitive with each other, comparing marks and being annoyed if a classmate does better than they do in a test. A little competition can give you extra motivation and encourage you to try harder.
>
> However, another way you can improve your skills is to **cooperate**, rather than compete, with each other. Share your favourite study methods. If you find how a friend learns interesting, write the idea down and try it out for yourself. If the technique works for you, add it to your personal study methods.
>
> Discussing the topics you are studying and your study methods helps to deepen and strengthen your understanding. This is particularly important in English, when there may not be simple 'right' or 'wrong' answers.
>
> Reflecting on your learning also helps you become more objective about your progress. You will think more clearly about how your skills are improving and the ways in which you want to develop them further.

Summary 11

Read the article about research into modern educational methods. Then write a summary explaining what classroom learning methods were found to be most popular with school students. Write about 100 words (and not more than 120 words). Use your own words as far as possible.

Pupils find internet 'a poor learning tool'

Schoolchildren believe they learn more from traditional methods, such as taking notes from the teacher, and reading the teacher's comments on their work, than they do from using the internet or watching videos, a government-funded study shows.

The findings will undermine the current trend to put information technology at the heart of learning. The present fashion is to put more and more of the curriculum online and to enable more schools to have faster access to the internet.

The government-funded survey, designed by pupils and carried out by the Science Museum, found that almost half of pupils thought that taking notes from the teacher was one of the most useful classroom activities.

Three-quarters of students said that watching videos was enjoyable but only a quarter of them thought it was effective. Fewer than one in ten rated the internet as useful. The report concluded that: 'The internet, though moderately enjoyable, is ranked very poorly as a learning tool.'

Research commissioned by the Association of Maintained Girls' Schools recently reported similar results. Academics at London Metropolitan University found that the 203 pupils questioned from eight schools valued contact with the teacher most highly. Fewer than a third of pupils said that learning through specially designed science and history computer courses was effective, compared with seventy per cent who said that opportunities to do practical work and listen to teacher explanations were essential.

At Kendrick Girls, a high-performing state school, computers are dotted around the school and pupils spend an hour a week learning how to master information and communications technology (ICT). Pupils, however, regard the internet's use across the curriculum as limited.

India Dhillon, 16, said: 'As I see it, the internet can be quite good but anyone can put anything on it, so you should not necessarily believe what you read. I learn most from listening and writing things down. Answering questions the teacher writes on the board is a good way to remember as well.' Jessica Burns, a classmate, valued textbooks specially written for her age group and doing revision tests set by the teacher. Quyen Hoang, 15, a pupil at King Edward VI school in Birmingham, said that material from the internet was often too easy or complex to be useful.

Children now use computers and the internet in every subject and from an early age. Groups of pupils gathered around a terminal looking at a monitor is a common sight in many classrooms. However, pupils complain that group work such as this can lead to some students not concentrating, distracting others, and generally 'messing around'.

Most headteachers think that there is a place for computers in the classroom but believe the teacher remains the most important resource. Lynn Gadd, the head of Copthall Girls' School in North London, said: 'In my opinion, you cannot put pupils in front of a computer and expect learning to happen by itself.'

Some critics also claim that multimedia approaches, including distance learning, e-learning, CD-ROMs and video, are being promoted as a solution to teacher shortages in the mistaken belief that students can access these resources independently and fewer teachers are required.

The Education Minister is not convinced by the criticisms. He believes that computers help teachers to be creative and engage pupils. 'Some people have a poor view of ICT in teaching and learning. I challenge that view.'

> **TIP** People named in a text
>
> When writing a summary, you often need to use information that was given by a particular person named in the original text. Sometimes the person's name is given and also their job title, nationality and maybe the organisation they work for. Referring to the status of the person is usually not necessary in a summary and uses up a lot of valuable words. Instead you should, if you can, extract only the key information that the person gives. Avoid giving exact quotes from a person's speech. It is better to try to put what they have said in your own words, as briefly as possible.

Note-taking 12

Read the article about ways to manage water supplies in the future and complete the notes under the headings given.

Thirsty work

More than seventy per cent of the world is covered with water in seas and oceans. The fact is, though, that ninety-seven per cent of water is too salty for use, and most of the fresh water in the world is too difficult to reach. Much of it is underground or frozen in icebergs. Only one per cent of the Earth's fresh water is readily available, but that, if managed properly, is plenty to meet the world's needs.

However, even this one per cent is sometimes unsafe to drink. Every day, 2 300 people die because their water is polluted by dangerous chemicals or untreated sewage. Diarrhoea, caused by dirty water and dirty conditions, kills more than 350 000 children a year through dehydration. Hundreds of millions of people suffer repeated bouts of diarrhoea which does not kill them but saps their energy and ability to work and grow food.

Governments are increasingly recognising that their nation's health is dependent on sanitation. The most successful schemes focus on involving a town or village in developing a supply of clean drinking water. Wells are often the best solution for a long-term, sustainable water supply.

The whole community is encouraged to take part in the planning and building of the well. The well is then maintained, mended and generally taken care of by local people without the need for outside help. The water pump, for example, sometimes breaks, but it can soon be fixed, as the community has been trained in doing repairs with inexpensive, easily available tools.

The schemes also aim to educate people about the need to avoid washing in contaminated water into which waste has been pumped. Where these schemes have been implemented, the well-being of the whole community has improved dramatically.

In addition to finding solutions to the problems of clean drinking water, experts are also considering ways to reduce the impact of water shortages on the world's food production. Already forty per cent of the world's population per cent of the world's population lives in countries where water is scarce. By 2030, one in five developing countries will be suffering from a water shortage. However, new agricultural techniques are being developed that can increase food production while using little water. By using better seeds and boosting soil fertility with the use of fertilisers, farmers can produce higher yields, obtaining the greatest gains from precious water supplies.

People's attitudes to water vary tremendously, according to the situation in which they live. In some regions, people have to manage with just one bucketful of water for a whole day. This means water for drinking, washing and cooking. On the other hand, in areas where people have a continuous supply of running water, they often use water wastefully and the concept of conserving water is a new one. For example, leaving the tap running while you brush your teeth uses 10 litres of water – the equivalent of a whole day's supply for some people.

Apart from developing better water management policies, many governments are now committed to awareness-raising campaigns, educating both adults and school children about responsible water use. The key to a future in which there is enough water for us all is a simple one: our water needs to be managed wisely, we all need to be careful with it, and we need to start today.

Why wells are a good way of providing a clean water supply

- ....
- ....
- ....
- ....

Ways of increasing food production where there is a water shortage

- ....
- ....

How education can help

- ....
- ....
- ....

Skills builder

Using the ideas in your notes, write a paragraph explaining the advantages of wells in bringing clean water to people. Write about 100 words (and not more than 120 words). Use your own words as far as possible.

> **TIP** **Help to prepare for examination**
>
> General interest topics are the kind of subjects you have studied in this book. Sometimes students say that they find these topics difficult as they have no personal experience of them in their everyday lives. If, for instance, you have good transport facilities in your area, it can be hard to imagine the many negative consequences of poor transport services. To help broaden your knowledge of topics, choose a subject which appeals to you and research it on interesting websites, by watching or listening to short factual programmes and reading relevant newspaper articles. Researching with a friend is fun and means you can also share your views with each other. Naturally, you won't understand all aspects of an unfamiliar topic instantly, so be patient and build up your knowledge step by step. Just spending a few minutes each day learning about a topic is enough and will make all the difference to your confidence. Whilst it is not possible to predict particular topics that might be set for an English language exam, all the topics should be of general interest for teenagers.

Summary 12

Read the article about the decline in minority languages. Then write a summary explaining how experts assess whether a language might disappear and why the girls want to preserve their traditional languages. Write about 100 words (and not more than 120 words). Use your own words as far as possible.

Lost for words

The Scottish island of Lewis, in a remote part of the British Isles, has two languages: English and the local language of Gaelic. In the village post office of Skigersta, little is spoken that isn't in Gaelic. There's Gaelic gossip and Gaelic small talk, and even the business is transacted in Gaelic – a sweet and lilting Celtic tongue.

But while older residents cling to Gaelic, each of the greeting cards in the post office is in English. 'Happy Anniversary' they shout and 'Well done! You've passed your exams!' For Gaelic is an endangered language, constantly threatened by English. Jayne, the 19-year-old daughter of the postmistress, says, 'Gaelic is definitely dying out. It seems to have an image problem among the youth and it's considered uncool and old-fashioned to speak it.'

Jayne, unlike many of her peers, has chosen to remain on Lewis and study for a BA in Gaelic language and culture. In her spare time, she organises traditional dancing classes, and she has taken part in a project to record the memories of older residents. She also hosts a radio programme in Gaelic.

In all of this, her inspiration comes from her grandmother, whose wealth of memories fascinates and motivates her. This close contact with the past has made Jayne realise how much will be lost if Gaelic dies out. 'It is so expressive', she says. 'There are sayings and phrases that just can't be translated into English. But it's not just that. The language and culture go hand in hand and it makes me sad to see them slipping away. It's part of my roots – part of my ancestry.'

UNESCO (United Nations Educational, Scientific and Cultural Organization) estimates the degree to which languages are under threat by looking at trends in language use. If thirty per cent of the children in a community no longer learn a language, then experts reckon it to be endangered. Around 3000 languages across the globe – half the world's languages – are thought to be in peril.

One of these is Sami. For thousands of years the Sami people were nomads whose way of life was based on reindeer husbandry around the Arctic Circle. Today, 80 000 Sami live in the extreme north of Europe, where their former herding grounds are divided between Norway, Sweden, Finland and Russia. Many modern Sami have rejected the old language in order to be progressive. This attitude appals 18-year-old Anna Karrstedt. She is at high school, and lives with her family in the Kiruna region of Sweden.

Where Jayne regards Gaelic as her first language, so Anna regards Sami as her mother tongue. Her enthusiasm for her ancestry and cultural heritage is also inspired by her grandmother, who has taught her many of the old skills associated with reindeer tending.

'I get so much joy out of being Sami and using the language', she says. 'I feel my Sami life is like an extra life. I would be so sad to see my language die out. I have my Swedish friends, but at the weekends I go off to the mountains with my uncle and get to be with the reindeer and with nature.'

These days, few young Sami or teenagers on Lewis expect to survive using the traditional skills, but both Jayne and Anna are determined to preserve their heritage. 'If there aren't any reindeer when my grandchildren are born, I would at least like to tell them how it was for me and my grandmother', says Anna. 'And, most of all, I would like to pass on the language'.

....	
....	
....	
....	
....	
....	
....	
....	
....	
....	
....	
....	
....	

> **TIP** Analysing correct answers
>
> Students sometimes say they feel rather disappointed with the marks they get for their practice notes and summaries, as they have been given lower marks than they were hoping for. They feel that they tackled the questions well and assumed they would get the highest marks. Often students are very close to the answer required, but unfortunately not quite close enough. The reason might be to do with the actual content chosen, or the way they have worded their answers.
>
> One way to see the difference between your own answer and the correct answer is to look at the corrections your teacher makes when giving work back. Another is to go through the right answers together in class and correct your own work. Whichever method you use, take a bit of time to study the differences between the correct answers and your own answers carefully, because often it is small changes that make the difference. You can also discuss with a friend the way you have worded your answers and compare notes. This is a good way to get further understanding of the wording or choices of content you have made.

Skills practice: Core level
Note-taking 13

Read the article about a people called the Huron-Wendat and make short notes under each heading.

The Huron-Wendat

The Huron-Wendat, (often called 'The Wendat'), are one of the 'First Nation' peoples of Canada, who have lived in North America for thousands of years. Before 1600, they numbered about 20 000 to 25 000 people, but between 1634 and 1642 they were reduced to about 9 000 by diseases brought to Canada by European settlers and traders. The Wendat lived in 18 to 25 villages, and some villages had up to 3 500 people.

We meet Natacha, a Wendat guide, who shows us around the re-creation of a historical village in the reservation of Wendake near Quebec City. In the past, Natacha explains, the Wendat lived in wooden structures known as longhouses, which were up to 90 metres long. Several families lived in each house and slept on raised wooden platforms, which they made comfortable with bear skins. The lower part of the longhouse was used for storage.

Older women were the heads of their families and made all the family decisions. Before any marriage could take place there would be a trial period when the man came to live with the woman's family for three weeks to make sure he would fit in. He brought the family gifts and, if the trial period did not work out, the family still kept the presents they had received.

The Wendat originally lived around a great lake that is now known as Lake Huron. The men were master boatbuilders who used wood from elm and birch trees to make canoes for hunting and fishing. They travelled by canoe to trade any surplus from their hunting and fishing expeditions. When the French arrived in the 17th century, the Wendat traded their furs with them.

The Wendat were also skilled farmers and grew about eighty per cent of what they ate. Beans, corn and squash were grown, and these three crops were called 'The Three Sisters'. Corn was planted in the centre as it provided a structure for the beans to climb up. The beans added nitrogen to the soil, which helped the plants to thrive. Squash were planted around the outside to stop weeds growing and their prickly leaves kept pests away.

Natacha tells us that living creatures were greatly respected. Animals and fish provided an important food source, and their body parts were used to help the Wendat survive and thrive. When animals were killed, tools were made from their claws, furs became blankets and holes in canoes were blocked by bear grease.

As well as being practical and resourceful, the Wendat believed in clear communication. On ceremonial occasions when many people gathered together, a wooden stick was passed around the group. It was called a 'talking stick' because you were allowed to speak only when you held it. Natacha tells us that it was an effective method for keeping order at special events. The stick was sacred to the Wendat and was blessed before use with the smoke of sacred herbs and other plants: sage, cedar, sweetgrass and tobacco. They decorated the stick with the parts of animals considered to be wise communicators. Geese bones were used, for instance, because these birds make clear calls.

Today the Wendat population is less than 3 000. They live a modern lifestyle and speak French as a first language. A third of the population live in Wendake.

Family life

- ....
- ....

(2 marks)

Attitude to animals and their uses to the Wendat

- ....
- ....

(2 marks)

The importance of the talking stick

- ....
- ....
- ....

(3 marks)

Total 7 marks

Summary 13

Read the internet article about a woman who is an author of travel books and blogs. Then write a summary giving advice about how to get the skills and attitudes that are useful for doing the job of a travel writer. Write about 80 words (and not more than 90 words). Use your own words as far as possible.

Travel writer

Many of our readers have told us they would love a career that took them to every continent on Earth. Luisa Texera's job involves travelling to exciting places around the world and writing books about the places she has visited. We asked Luisa to tell us about her work and whether she had any tips for would-be travel writers of the future.

'I am doing my dream job but it is not always easy', says Luisa. 'On the first day of one trip, I was sailing around islands in Alaska when a fierce storm blew up. I almost panicked but I told myself it was an adventure and that I would manage. So the first thing I would say if you want to write travel books is that you should have an adventurous approach to unpredictable situations.' Fortunately, Luisa's positive attitude led to a successful outcome and she completed her trip safely.

Luisa enjoys writing true stories about her journeys through the world's most difficult terrain. 'I have climbed mountains in New Zealand, hiked through the rainforest in Costa Rica, and crossed India and Sri Lanka on a bicycle', says Luisa. 'I look for ways to interest my readers in places they may never have heard of.' She explains that writing is a craft. 'I recommend that you develop strong writing skills as I know from experience that it is vital to engage readers and keep them reading.'

Luisa feels there are many ways to broaden our knowledge of different cultures and customs even while we still live at home. 'Watch interesting travel shows on television and read lots of books and magazines to get inspiration about places you would love to visit.'

Says Luisa, 'Wherever I have been, I have had memorable conversations with amazing people. I suggest you make the effort to learn foreign languages, as building close relationships makes all the difference.' She adds, 'People I meet teach me how to see the world differently.'

Finally, Luisa believes you should never let self-doubt stop you. 'Always be persistent and make your dreams a reality.'

(12 marks)

Note-taking 14

Read the article about the use of robots in the workplace. Then write short notes under each heading.

The rise of the robot

In 1961, the American vehicle manufacturer, General Motors, installed the first robotic device in order to make car production more efficient. Since then, robots have been used in factories all over the world to save time and reduce costs. In fact, experts say robots can improve productivity fourfold. Increasingly, human workers have had to learn how to work with robotic devices. For example, in a modern factory, a robot might be used to carry a box of tools to employees, who then select the tool they need for their work.

Modern robots have sophisticated sensors that can 'see', 'touch' and have better balance. 'Baxter', for example, is a type of robot that can automatically move around a factory without bumping into the workers. If something unexpected happens, Baxter is programmed to react safely so there is no danger to people.

The first attempts at artificial intelligence – to create machines that could 'think' – began in 1956 when scientists first met to explore ways a machine might be programmed to use language, solve problems or form abstract concepts. In practice, developments in artificial intelligence were slow. The belief that it would not be long before every home would have a robot 'housework helper' that would cook dinner, make beds, wash up and take the children to school was proved to be wrong.

In the last few years, however, scientists' understanding of artificial intelligence has sped up significantly and computer programmers are now able to program robots to do things that require advanced levels of 'thinking'. Programs are being developed, for instance, that enable robots to detect and remove unwanted spam emails from computer inboxes. A robot can now recognise people by their individual characteristics so it can identify a person in a photo posted on social media. Programmers also claim a robot is as good as an experienced lawyer in predicting what kind of legal argument is most likely to succeed in court. In other words, robots' 'brains' are being developed to be more like human brains.

Some people suggest that artificial intelligence is worrying because it takes the power of the machine to a completely new level. Whilst people always feared machines might destroy jobs, the jobs that were lost because of technology were usually done by hand. In the 19th century, for example, a group of English hand weavers known as 'Luddites' broke weaving machines as they feared the machines would destroy their craft. Until recently, the trend was that when jobs were lost, new sorts of jobs were created.

Now, however, we are in a situation of having machines that can think faster than people so robots can, increasingly, replace the 'thinking' part of jobs of all types. 'Robotic headsets', for instance, are being designed to be worn by factory workers. The headsets dictate, for example, how many items should be packed into a box and workers follow these orders step by step. However, even with the latest hardware, a robot cannot be programmed to clean a toilet because of the range of movements and physical agility needed for that task.

If the robots of the future will be used to carry out intellectual functions, what kind of work will be left for people? Jobs like cleaning toilets? We will see.

Benefits of robots in the workplace

- ....
- ....

(2 marks)

Examples of robots' recent 'thinking' jobs

- ....
- ....
- ....

(3 marks)

Effects on our jobs in the future

- ....
- ....

(2 marks)

Total 7 marks

Summary 14

Read the article about laughter. Then write a summary outlining the physical and mental benefits of laughter. Write about 80 words (and not more than 90 words). Use your own words as far as possible.

Laughter: the best medicine

Laughter coach Luka Lipsi is not a clown, but his job is to make people laugh. He says, 'Businesses engage me to work with their staff on team-building days. Once colleagues learn to laugh together they become more like friends, not just professional associates.' He believes the positive feeling the staff get from laughing with each other improves the amount and quality of work enormously.

Experts say children laugh 300–400 times a day but adults laugh only 15–20 times a day. Luka thinks that's a shame. He teaches his trainees a physical technique that starts them laughing naturally. He says, 'Once people use my method, they are surprised how easy it is to laugh. In fact, some people laugh so much they find it difficult to stop.'

Dr John Li, a psychologist doing laughter research in California, USA, insists that every time we laugh we release hormones that help our muscles to relax. We also breathe out stale air and breathe in more oxygen, which gives us energy.

In one of his experiments, John asked volunteers to watch a popular half-hour comedy programme on television. The levels of their stress hormones were measured before and after the show. 'The programme was very funny and my volunteers laughed all the way through it. The measurements taken showed the reduction in their stress hormones was the same as if they had spent 30 minutes working out in the gym.'

John's research also suggests that laughter helps us live longer as it increases the immune response. We are less likely to get cancer or suffer from harmful viruses.

Marchin Nowak is a Polish clown who works for a medical charity. He performs in hospitals for sick children and their families. 'My work is so rewarding', he says. 'Audiences tell me that I give them hope.'

Marchin also shares the view of laughter experts when he adds that laughter is the foundation of his happy marriage to his wife Magda. 'We laugh together and share private jokes. When I am feeling down, laughing with Magda gives me perspective. I know I am a lucky man.'

(12 marks)

Skills practice: Extended level
Note-taking 15

Read the article about a people called the Huron-Wendat and make short notes under each heading.

The Huron-Wendat

The Huron-Wendat, (often called 'The Wendat'), are one of the 'First Nation' peoples of Canada, who have lived in North America for thousands of years. Before 1600, they numbered about 20 000 to 25 000 people, but between 1634 and 1642 they were reduced to about 9 000 by diseases brought to Canada by European settlers and traders. The Wendat lived in 18 to 25 villages, and some villages had up to 3500 people.

We meet Natacha, a Wendat guide, who shows us around the re-creation of a historical village in the reservation of Wendake near Quebec City. In the past, Natacha explains, the Wendat lived in wooden structures known as longhouses, which were up to 90 metres long. Several families lived in each house and slept on raised wooden platforms, which they made comfortable with bear skins. The lower part of the longhouse was used for storage.

Older women were the heads of their families and made all the family decisions. Before any marriage could take place there would be a trial period when the man came to live with the woman's family for three weeks to make sure he would fit in. He brought the family gifts and, if the trial period did not work out, the family still kept the presents they had received.

The Wendat originally lived around a great lake that is now known as Lake Huron. The men were master boatbuilders who used wood from elm and birch trees to make canoes for hunting and fishing. They travelled by canoe to trade any surplus from their hunting and fishing expeditions. When the French arrived in the 17th century, the Wendat traded their furs with them.

The Wendat were also skilled farmers and grew about eighty per cent of what they ate. Beans, corn and squash were grown, and these three crops were called 'The Three Sisters'. Corn was planted in the centre as it provided a structure for the beans to climb up. The beans added nitrogen to the soil, which helped the plants to thrive. Squash were planted around the outside to stop weeds growing and their prickly leaves kept pests away.

Natacha tells us that living creatures were greatly respected. Animals and fish provided an important food source, and their body parts were used to help the Wendat survive and thrive. When animals were killed, tools were made from their claws, furs became blankets and holes in canoes were blocked by bear grease.

As well as being practical and resourceful, the Wendat believed in clear communication. On ceremonial occasions when many people gathered together, a wooden stick was passed around the group. It was called a 'talking stick' because you were allowed to speak only when you held it. Natacha tells us that it was an effective method for keeping order at special events. The stick was sacred to the Wendat and was blessed before use by the smoke of sacred herbs and other plants: sage, cedar, sweetgrass and tobacco. They decorated the stick with the parts of animals considered to be wise communicators. Geese bones were used, for instance, because these birds make clear calls.

Today the Wendat population is less than 3 000. They live a modern lifestyle and speak French as a first language. A third of the population live in Wendake.

Family life

- ....
- ....
- ....

(3 marks)

Attitude to animals and their uses to the Wendat

- ....
- ....
- ....

(3 marks)

The importance of the talking stick

- ....
- ....
- ....

(3 marks)

Total 9 marks

Summary 15

Read the internet article about Suzi who cared for a serval (a wild cat found in Africa). Then write a summary outlining what Suzi did to raise him AND enable him to live normally in the wild. Write about 100 words (and not more than 120 words). Use your own words as far as possible.

Serval rescue

When park rangers from the Maasai Mara National Reserve in Kenya contacted Suzi to ask her to care for a serval, she didn't know what to expect. The rangers explained to her that they had been burning the vegetation on the savannah (a routine job which keeps these grasslands healthy) when the serval became separated from its mother. They guessed that the mother, sensing danger, had begun moving each of her newborn kittens to safety, when this kitten got lost. Suzi, a wildlife photographer who camps on the reserve, says, 'I think he was about a week old and his eyes were just beginning to open. As there is no wildlife hospital on the reserve, the rangers asked me to look after him.'

The newborn wild cat reminded her of a tiny leopard and she named him Moto, which means 'Fire' in Swahili. She says, 'I would have loved to keep him at home as my little pet but decided to raise him to return to a normal adult life on the savannah.'

Moto was underweight and dehydrated so Suzi's first job was to help him eat. She downloaded recipes for making serval milk formula, and used a human baby bottle to feed him by hand. Although she fed him every three hours, including at night, Suzi noticed the cat was getting thinner. He seemed sad and uninterested. Feeling worried, she sought help from a wildlife specialist who advised her to let Moto hear her heartbeat and feel her skin, just as if he was with his real mother. Suzi was unsure how to do that until she got the idea of sewing extra pockets onto her shirts, which meant she could carry Moto around all the time and keep him close. To imitate the comforting stroke of a serval mother's rough tongue, she brushed his fur with a toothbrush. Brushing was simple but effective. He loved it.

The next stage was to encourage Moto to walk, so she put him on the ground outside and he soon became confident at walking. Realising that in the wild Moto would have played with other kittens, Suzi gave him a little toy duck to have fun with. Later, as his hunting instincts developed, Moto practised stalking, jumping and pouncing, just as if the soft toy were real prey.

When he was six weeks old, Suzi began feeding him dead rats. This helped prepare Moto for hunting the rodents, which servals naturally enjoy eating. As servals hunt at night, Suzi opened her tent door to encourage him to explore after dark. He came back when it was light and slept next to her.

Eventually, Suzi assumed he was hunting confidently as he was not hungry for the food she gave him and his personality became wilder and more aggressive. Suzi says, 'He stopped sleeping in the tent. After six months, he completely disappeared. I feared he had been attacked and killed.'

A couple of weeks later, a park ranger visited and told Suzi that he had encountered a serval, which nuzzled his leg. He looked down and immediately recognised Moto, looking healthy and strong. 'I was so happy and proud', says Suzi. 'But there's no way what I did for him was as good as what his real mum would have done.'

(16 marks)

Note-taking 16

Read the article about the use of robots in the workplace. Then write short notes under each heading.

The rise of the robot

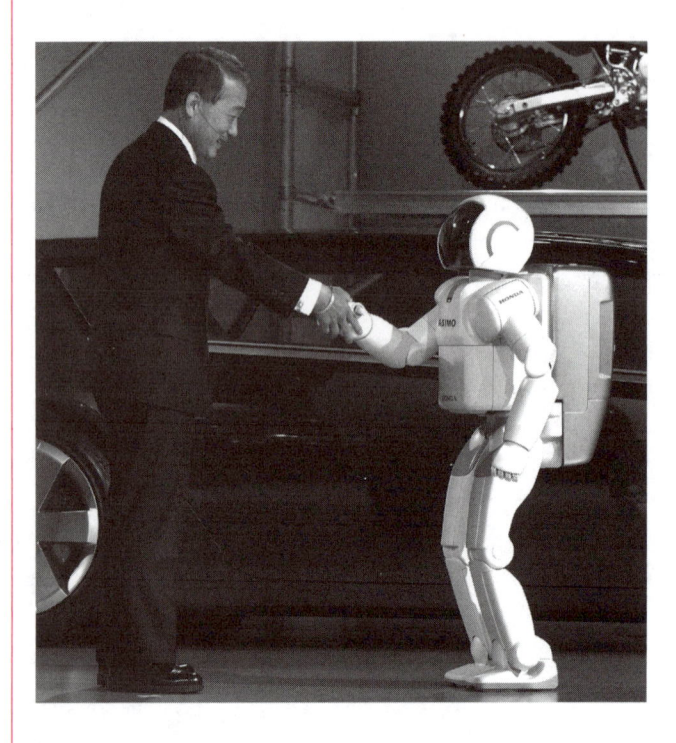

In 1961, the American vehicle manufacturer General Motors installed the first robotic device in order to make car production more efficient. Since then, robots have been used in factories all over the world to save time and reduce costs. In fact, experts say robots can improve productivity fourfold. Increasingly, human workers have had to learn how to work with robotic devices. For example, in a modern factory, a robot might be used to carry a box of tools to employees, who then select the tool they need for their work.

Modern robots have sophisticated sensors that can 'see', 'touch' and have better balance. 'Baxter', for example, is a type of robot that can automatically move around a factory without bumping into the workers. If something unexpected happens, Baxter is programmed to react safely so there is no danger to people.

The first attempts at artificial intelligence – to create machines that could 'think' – began in 1956 when scientists first met to explore ways a machine might be programmed to use language, solve problems or form abstract concepts. In practice, developments in artificial intelligence were slow. The belief that it would not be long before every home would have a robot 'housework helper' that would cook dinner, make beds, wash up and take the children to school was proved to be wrong.

In the last few years, however, scientists' understanding of artificial intelligence has speeded up significantly and computer programmers are now able to program robots to do things which require advanced levels of 'thinking'. Programs are being developed, for instance, which enable robots to detect and remove unwanted spam emails from computer inboxes. A robot can now recognise people by their individual characteristics, so it can identify a person in a photo posted on social media. Programmers also claim a robot is as good as an experienced lawyer in predicting what kind of legal argument is most likely to succeed in court. In other words, robots' 'brains' are being developed to be more like human brains.

Some people suggest that artificial intelligence is worrying because it takes the power of the machine to a completely new level. Whilst people always feared machines might destroy jobs, the jobs that were lost because of technology were usually done by hand. In the 19th century, for example, a group of English hand weavers known as 'Luddites' broke weaving machines as they feared the machines would destroy their craft. Until recently, the trend was that when jobs were lost, new sorts of jobs were created.

Now, however, we are in a situation of having machines that can think faster than people so robots can, increasingly, replace the 'thinking' part of jobs of all types. 'Robotic headsets', for instance, are being designed to be worn by factory workers. The headsets dictate how many items should be packed into a box and workers follow these orders step by step. However, even with the latest hardware, a robot cannot be programmed to clean a toilet because of the range of movements and physical agility needed for that task.

If the robots of the future will be used to carry out intellectual functions, what kind of work will be left for people? Jobs like cleaning toilets? We will see.

Benefits of robots in the workplace

- ....
- ....
- ....

(3 marks)

Examples of robots' recent 'thinking' jobs

- ....
- ....
- ....

(3 marks)

Effects on our jobs in the future

- ....
- ....
- ....

(3 marks)

Total 9 marks

Summary 16

Read the talk given by an astronaut about his time in outer space. Then write a summary of what helps astronauts adapt to life on board the International Space Station. Write about 100 words (and not more than 120 words). Use your own words as far as possible.

Space mission

Good morning everyone and thank you for coming today. I have wonderful memories I'd like to share with you of my time at the International Space Station – a satellite laboratory in space, 400 kilometres above the Earth. We call it the ISS.

One experience I shall never forget was the first time after the spacecraft took off when my arms rose up by themselves and floated in front of me. It showed we were at zero gravity. After three years of intensive preparation, we had finally blasted into space. Our space mission was underway at last and we had left Earth far behind.

When we arrived at the ISS, we docked our spacecraft and floated into the space station. Colleagues were waiting to greet us with lots of smiles and hugs. People ask how I coped with being in space, so far from friends and family. My answer was 'My team'. Not only were they supportive and kind, but we had lots of fun together. And, of course, I had had three years of special training to be an astronaut.

Living at zero gravity is strange but amazing and we gradually got used to the unique living arrangements. Everything in the ISS has to be fixed in place or it will float around. Even using the toilet requires a foot restraint and a seat belt! Sleeping is totally different as it is impossible to lie down in a bed at zero gravity. We used special sleeping bags, which were surprisingly comfortable as they had holes for our arms to stick out and float as we slept. The ISS is divided into quarters and we slept in a space the size of a broom cupboard. In the mornings we couldn't shower (water sticks to you in space), but wiped ourselves clean with a damp washcloth. No excuses for anyone being smelly!

To create a sense of normality, we followed a structured routine based on Greenwich Meantime (GMT), which is the time in Greenwich, London. GMT is halfway between Russian and American time zones, so it suited our team. We worked from 8 a.m. to 7 p.m. during the week and had evenings and weekends free. Work was important on the mission and we made good use of our time. We did experiments in the laboratory, which is the most hi-tech environment imaginable.

One project focused on how to grow food in space. As space exploration develops, there are plans to travel further into space and be away for longer so we need food supplies that are sustainable. On the mission, we ate dehydrated food mixed with water. It's reassuring that it's nutritionally well balanced, but this kind of food is unexciting. On someone's birthday, we allowed ourselves a fresh orange or apple, which was a real treat to enjoy slowly.

After work, we relaxed, emailed or called our loved ones. I enjoyed playing my guitar. I'm not a very good musician but my friends were very tolerant! Then we had the most unforgettable views, including seeing the sun rise over and over again in a 24-hour period. The speed of the spacecraft meant we orbited the Earth sixteen times each day! That experience compensates anyone for being away from home for six months at a time!

(16 marks)

Topic vocabulary and writing task
Note-taking 1: Tackling dyslexia in children

Topic vocabulary

Group A
dyslexia
dyslexic
process visual information
eye movement / wobble
focus on

Group B
trouble reading
trouble writing
lack of eye control
reading difficulties
the printed page

Group C
glare
headache
disturbing sensation
rub your eyes

Group D
area of the brain
brain difference
cell

Group E
scientist
professor
patient
clinic

Group F
tests
assess
research
connection between

Group G
adapt
develop

Vocabulary challenge 1

Add the following words and phrases to the best three groups in the vocabulary list above. (They are **not** taken from the text.)

- eye strain
- medical centre
- written word

Writing task 1

Your class recently attended a careers event at a science research centre. Write a report for your headteacher about the visit. Here are some comments your friends posted about the visit.

'The professor explained some of the amazing research she has done.'

'There was not enough time to look around the laboratories.'

'A research career is for me! I am going to work harder at my science subjects.'

'The talks were too long and difficult to understand.'

Write a report giving your own views. The comments above may give you ideas but you should try to use some ideas of your own. Use the topic vocabulary feature to help you. Write 150–200 words.

Summary 1: All in the mind?

Topic vocabulary

Group A
personal healing powers
dramatic effects on the patient's condition
positive physical changes

Group B
an inert substance
no active ingredients

Group C
fake medicine
to cheat
unethical
placebo

Group D
clinical trials
research studies

Group E
good results
a successful outcome

Group F
fatty food
high-calorie treats
food cravings
to snack

Group G
hunger pangs
appetite
to eat in moderation
nutritious meals

Group H
trim shape
glowing skin
glossy hair
radiantly healthy

Group I
to comfort
to reassure
to praise

Group J
to perceive
to believe
to expect

Group K
to imagine
to visualise
to picture

Group L
gorgeous trouser suit
stylish clothes

Group M
self-respect
self-esteem

Vocabulary challenge 2

Choose a word or expression from two or three of the groups and write a sentence to show its meaning.

Writing task 2

Your friend has written to you asking for advice. They would like to lose a little weight and be healthier.
Write an email to encourage them to reach their goal. In your email you should:

- praise them for their decision
- suggest some changes they could make to get slimmer and healthier
- explain how positive thinking could help.

Use the topic vocabulary feature to help you. Write 150–200 words.

....

....

....

Note-taking 2: Antibiotic resistance

Topic vocabulary

Group A
common illnesses
bacterial infections
viral infection
infectious diseases
infection-related deaths

Group B
to suffer from
suffering

Group C
to fight off
to overcome

Group D
curable
to cure

Group E
to prescribe
a prescription

Group F
a variety
a wide range

Group G
to get better
to get over
to recover

Group H
difficult to treat
complex treatment
resistant to antibiotics

Group I
medication
tablets
drugs
in liquid form

Group J
pharmaceutical companies
scientists

Group K
a matter of time
speeded up
accelerating

Vocabulary challenge 3

Choose a word or expression from two or three of the groups above and write a sentence to show its meaning.

Writing task 3

Your local health centre issues this notice:
The health centre is planning to reduce the number of prescriptions given to patients, especially for antibiotics.
Here are some comments from your friends about this idea.

'Being ill is horrible. This action will make people suffer more and for longer.'

'We can get over lots of illnesses ourselves without treatment.'

'I can't waste time being unwell. I need to have antibiotics so I can get on with my life.'

'We are at risk from superbugs because too many antibiotics have been prescribed.'

Write an email to the health centre giving your views. The comments above may give you some ideas but you should try to use ideas of your own. Use the topic vocabulary feature to help you.

....

....

Summary 2: The enemy within

Topic vocabulary

Group A
allergy
allergic reaction
allergic to
sufferer
food allergy

Group B
disorder
asthma
hay fever
trigger a reaction
severe reaction

Group C
immune system
virus
parasite
micro-organism
harmless substance
antibody
histamine
chemicals

Group D
inflame the tissues
attach itself to

Group E
allergen
pollen
nuts
peanuts
strawberries
wasp / bee sting
processed food
additive
colouring

Group F
swelling
rash
sneezing
sore eyes
breathlessness
anaphylaxis

Group G
lifestyle
double glazing
central heating

Group H
find a cure
control symptoms
medicine
avoid contact with

Vocabulary challenge 4

Find the verbs and verb phrases in the list above and add 'to' in front of each one. Then write two or three example sentences to show their meaning.

Writing task 4

You were enjoying a special family party when you had an allergic reaction for the first time to something you ate. Write an email to a friend in which you explain:

- why the party was taking place
- what happened when you had the allergic reaction
- how other people reacted
- what treatment you had, if any
- how you are feeling now.

Use the topic vocabulary feature to help you. Write 150–200 words.

Note-taking 3: The thrill of watching whales

Topic vocabulary

Group A	**Group D**	**Group G**
cetaceans	marine environment	record details
whale	submerged rocks	environmental
porpoise	underwater	conditions
dolphin	land	distribution
fin	shore	

Group B
sea creature
sea life
marine life
flock of seabirds
wild animal

Group E
detect
see
distinguish between
differentiate

Group H
patient
peaceful
quiet
tranquillity
undisturbed

Group C
current
tide
wave
break
splash

Group F
sighting
pair of binoculars

Group I
take your time
sit quietly

Vocabulary challenge 5

The prefix 'sub' sometimes means 'below' or 'less than'. 'Submerged rocks' means rocks that are below the surface of the water. Write two or three more words that begin with the prefix 'sub'. Use a dictionary if you need to.

Writing task 5

You recently enjoyed a holiday by the sea and were lucky enough at times to see some interesting sea life. Write an email to a friend describing your holiday. Don't forget to include:

- where you went on holiday
- what you enjoyed about the holiday
- details of the sea life you observed
- why your friend might enjoy a holiday like this too.

Use the topic vocabulary feature to help you. Write 150–200 words.

Summary 3: Why zoo cats lose their cool

Topic vocabulary

Group A
big cat
lion
tiger
feline
cub

Group B
monkey
gorilla
chimpanzee
primate
species

Group C
cleaning themselves
licking themselves
grooming

Group D
abnormal / strange
  behaviour
disturbed behaviour
stressed
irritated

Group E
active
vigilant
on the alert
on guard

Group F
suspicious
watchful
pace back and forth
pace / move around
prick up their ears

Group G
asleep
resting
yawning
nocturnal

Group H
welfare
well-being
health
quality of life

Group I
zoo keeper
visitor
enclosure

Group J
attract their
  attention
wave
call
make noise

Vocabulary challenge 6

Add the following words and phrases to the best three groups in the vocabulary list above. (They are **not** taken from the text.)

- lying down
- elephant
- cage

Writing task 6

You recently visited a local zoo and were sorry to see large animals appearing restless and unhappy. Write an email to the zoo manager describing your visit and suggesting some ways the zoo could improve the care of the animals. Don't forget to include:

- details of when you made the visit
- examples of distress in the animals
- examples of ways some of the visitors were disturbing the animals
- your suggestions for ways the care of the animals could be improved.

Use the topic vocabulary feature to help you. Write 150–200 words.

Note-taking 4: The secret world of polar bears

Topic vocabulary

Group A
polar bear
seal

Group B
skin
blubber
layer of fat
mouth
fur
paw print

Group C
fresh snow
ice
waterhole
surroundings

Group D
protect
look after

Group E
unique characteristics
sex
eye colour
individual
size

Group F
underground shelter
den
entrance

Group G
cells
genetic code
hereditary information
DNA

Group H
heat
rise in temperature
warm
bitterly cold

Group I
team of scientists
conservation workers
laboratories
test
results
samples
analyse

Vocabulary challenge 7

Add the following words and phrases to the best three groups in the vocabulary list above. (They are not taken from the text.)

- experiment
- age
- home

Writing task 7

You are a member of the school Nature Club. Recently your club attended a talk given by a scientist who had been working on a project in the Arctic to protect polar bears. The school management committee has asked you to write a report giving the Nature Club's opinions of the talk. Here are some comments from your friends at the Nature Club:

'We learned a lot about what the project has achieved in the Arctic.'

'The equipment wasn't working so we couldn't see the video she had brought to show us.'

'It was amazing! We want to visit the Arctic and see these fabulous animals ourselves.'

'We didn't learn anything about how scientists cope with living in the Arctic. It was disappointing not to hear about how they got food or kept warm.'

Write a report for the committee giving your views. The comments here may give you ideas but you should try to use some ideas of your own. Use the topic vocabulary feature to help you. Write 150–200 words.

Summary 4: Undercover cats

Topic vocabulary

Group A
a dense habitat
forest
scrubland
mangrove

Group B
bushy cover
a safe corridor of scrubland
the brush

Group C
farmers
landowners
agricultural organisations

Group D
to mix
to find mates
to reproduce
inbreeding

Group E
to tranquilise
to drug
drowsy

Group F
conservation-minded
conservationists
to preserve

Group G
an endangered species
to save from extinction
magnificent creatures

Group H
a small population
survival
to survive
to flourish

Vocabulary challenge 8

Choose between six and ten words or phrases from the list and learn to spell them correctly. The best method is to study each word, take a mental 'photograph' and then write the word out. Finally, check your spelling to make sure the word is correct. If not, repeat the process.

Writing task 8

Your headteacher is considering asking school students to raise funds to support a conservation programme to save an endangered species in another part of the world. As you are the leader of the wildlife club, the headteacher has asked you to write a report saying whether you think this is a good idea. Here are some comments about the idea from your friends at the club:

'Supporting a conservation programme to protect the pandas would be a great idea.'

'I would prefer to help our local animal sanctuary care for small birds and animals.'

'Supporting a breeding programme to increase the numbers of endangered species would be very worthwhile.'

'Raising money is hard work. This year we should concentrate on preparing for exam success.'

Write a report for the headteacher giving your views. The comments above may give you ideas but you should try to use some ideas of your own. Use the topic vocabulary feature to help you. Write 150–200 words.

Note-taking 5: A natural antiseptic

Topic vocabulary

Group A
tea tree oil
tea tree plantation
conifer
bush
bark
needles
spikes
bushy plant

Group B
seeds
germinate
seedlings

Group C
growing process
transplant
greenhouse /
  glasshouse
irrigation
watering
pricking-out
weeding

Group D
labour intensive
casual labour

Group E
distillation process
steam

Group F
evaporate
vapour
water-cooled
  condenser
separator
draw off
fluid
process of extraction

Group G
tray
container
bin
drum
stainless steel

Group H
pharmacy
health food shop

Group I
acne
dry, itchy skin
bruises
burns
dermatitis
fungal infection
antiseptic
antibacterial agent

Vocabulary challenge 9

What is the difference in meaning between:

- *seeds* and *seedlings*?
- *fluid* and *steam*?

Look back the text and also use a dictionary if you need to.

Writing task 9

COMPETITION!

Buzz magazine wants to find out which skincare products its readers use. Let us know about the product you prefer and why, and we'll print the best articles. The lucky winners will also receive a whole basket of skincare products **or** six DVDs and CDs of their choice.

You see this competition in a teenage magazine and decide to submit an entry. In your article you could include:

- why teenage skin can be problematic
- good methods for caring for teenage skin
- which skincare product you use and why
- whether you would recommend this product to other teenagers.

Use the topic vocabulary feature to help you. Write 150–200 words.

Summary 5: The rose, queen of all flowers

Topic vocabulary

Group A
grow
cultivate
mass cultivation
agricultural product
favourable climate
hybrid
botanist

Group B
flower
bloom
root
stem
leaves
petals
thorns
sharp / prickly

Group C
colour
scent
fragrance

Group D
rose petals
grain of pollen
preserved / dried flowers

Group E
ancient graves / tombs
burial ceremony

Group F
appreciated
highly valued
popularity
romantic gift

Group G
transportation
lucrative market
all over the world
rose-growing business

Group H
symbolise
rich symbolism
preserved / dried flowers

Vocabulary challenge 10

Tick (✓) any words or expressions in the vocabulary list that you already know from subjects other than English.

Writing task 10

A rich citizen of your town died recently. He left the town a sum of money to improve the town park, and your town council has asked local people to suggest ways this could be done. You think planting a rose garden would be a good idea. Write an email to your local newspaper giving your views. Your email should cover:

- where in the park the rose garden should be planted
- why a rose garden would improve the park
- how local people might use it
- why the rose has always been a special and popular flower.

Use the topic vocabulary feature to help you. Write 150–200 words.

....

....

....

....

Note-taking 6: Sweet talk

Topic vocabulary

Group A
botanical name
cocoa tree
cocoa plantation
cocoa bean
cocoa butter
leathery pod
made from

Group B
good for the heart
spots
migraine
obesity
stressed-out
nerves

Group C
irresistible foodstuff
one of the world's favourite foods

Group D
crush
boil
add spices
tasty, frothy drink
grind into a powder
heat
sweeten
press into a mould
melt

Group E
solid chocolate
bar of chocolate
chocolate

Group F
meet the growing demand
more easily available
short shelf life

Group G
chemist
food scientist

Vocabulary challenge 11

Add the following words and phrases to the best three groups in the vocabulary list above. (They are **not** taken from the text.)

- add sugar
- delicious
- doctor

Writing task 11

Report for the headteacher

This year your class raised money to help a charity for sick children by selling chocolate items. You and your classmates decided to make items from chocolate and sell them during the school breaks. Your headteacher has asked for a report on the fundraising day, saying whether the event should be repeated for next year's group. Here are some comments from your friends, giving their views.

'We made the biscuits and sweets in in the school kitchen. Everyone said they were delicious.'

'It was too much effort to cook and clean up afterwards.'

'We cooperated well with each other. I am proud of what we did.'

'We only made $32 profit for the charity. Next time, we should have a fund-raising walk.'

Write a report for the headteacher giving your views. The comments on page 86 may give you ideas but you should use some ideas of your own. Use the topic vocabulary feature to help you. Write 150–200 words.

Summary 6: The mangoes in your trolley

Topic vocabulary

Group A
wild mangoes
mango tree
mango crop
mango producer

Group B
tropical fruit
tropical country
the tropics
temperate climate

Group C
global market
lucrative

Group D
gain popularity
grow in popularity

Group E
high nutritional value
good source of
 vitamins
protein
fructose
fibre
delicious
sweet, juicy flesh

Group F
variable in quality
below the standard
 required

Group G
propagation
select
reject
good quality fruit
best quality seedlings

Group H
travel well
air freight / transport
minimum delay
in storage
refrigeration

Group I
deteriorate
over-ripe
unfit for sale

Group J
supermarket shelves
shoppers
pay extra
at its best

Vocabulary challenge 12

Add the following words and phrases to the best three groups in the vocabulary list above. (They are **not** taken from the text.)

- customers
- overseas sales
- good for health

Writing task 12

Do you like fruit?

Our school survey has found that lots of us are not eating enough fruit! If you enjoy fruit, we'd like to hear from you, especially if you like eating more unusual varieties.
All articles to the School Newsletter Editor by **Friday**, please.

You like fruit and decide to submit an article for the school newsletter explaining why. In your article you should say:

- what kinds of fruit you like eating
- what you look for when you buy fruit

- why fruit is good for you
- why your friends should try some new kinds of fruit.

Use the topic vocabulary feature to help you. Write 150–200 words.

Note-taking 7: Lost on the mountain

Topic vocabulary

Group A
mountain
jungle
dense rainforest
gorge
swamp
stream
waterfall
slope
ridge
rocky gully
thick vegetation

Group B
infested with
poisonous snakes
vines
tendrils
lacerate bare skin

Group C
survive
survival
remarkable escape

Group D
weather conditions
unusually warm and dry

Group E
injured
scratched
cut
bruised
unarmed
ordeal

Group F
helicopter
search party
in groups of four
armed with
 walkie-talkies
keep close together
hard to find
out in the open
failure to spot her

Group G
resourceful
calm
terrified
exhausted
dumbfounded

Group H
clamber over boulders
hack through the
 undergrowth
loose rocks underfoot

Vocabulary challenge 13

Distinguish between two or three of the following pairs of words or phrases in the word lists above.

- *swamp* and *stream*
- *scratched* and *bruised*
- *clamber over boulders* and *hack through the undergrowth*

Writing task 13

On a recent school camping holiday, two of the younger children got lost. You took part in the search party that eventually found them safe and well. Write an email to a friend describing the experience. In your email you should say:

- what the search party did
- where you were camping and why
- what happened when everyone realised the children were missing
- what happened in the end.

Use the topic vocabulary feature to help you. Write 150–200 words.

Summary 7: Young ambassadors

Topic vocabulary

Group A
a year abroad / overseas
host country
home university
different community

Group B
undergraduate
language student
overseas / foreign university

Group C
culture shock
culture

Group D
perseverance
willingness to fit in
open-mindedness
determination

Group E
get insights into
responsibilities

Group F
attend lectures
do coursework
complete an assignment
improve academic skills

Group G
keep in touch
maintain contact
give support
keep informed

Group H
personal tutor
lecture
checklist
guide
handbook
web-based information
questionnaire

Vocabulary challenge 14

Add the following words and phrases to the best three groups in the vocabulary list above. (They are **not** taken from the text.)

- send a text
- take exams
- courage

Writing task 14

As part of your studies, your school is considering starting a Study Abroad scheme. Students will spend one month in another part of the world, living with a family, attending the local school and visiting places of interest.

As a student representative on the school management committee, you have been asked whether you think this is a good idea. Here are some comments from your friends, giving their views:

'We will gain insights into another culture.'

'We would concentrate much better by staying at home.'

'It will make us more confident and open-minded.'

'One whole month so far away in another part of the world would be too lonely.'

Write a report for the school management committee giving your views. The comments on page 92 may give you ideas but you should try to use some ideas of your own. Use the topic vocabulary feature to help you. Write 150–200 words.

Note-taking 8: Taking a gap year

Topic vocabulary

Group A
exam results
place at university

Group B
year out
gap year
trip
foreign expedition
see the world
thousands of
  kilometres away

Group C
backpacking
mountaineering
trekking

Group D
fare and expenses
meet the target

Group E
skills
personal qualities

Group F
daunting
hard work
nerve-wracking

Group G
stunning
incredible
inspiring

Group H
tolerance
accept other people
consider other people
help each other
make you less selfish

Group I
distracted from your
  studies
concentrate
analyse information

Vocabulary challenge 15

Add the following words to the best three groups in the vocabulary list above. (They are **not** taken from the text.)

- abilities
- amazing
- difficult

Writing task 15

Is a 'gap year' between school and university a good idea, or is it a waste of time? Here are some comments made by young people about the concept:

'A gap year helps you grow up and become more mature.'

'You don't achieve anything in a gap year – you just laze around.'

'It's an opportunity to have a break from studying and do something really different.'

'If you travel in a gap year it's very expensive. I'd rather use the money to help with my studies.'

Write an article for the school magazine expressing **your** views on a gap year. The comments above may give you ideas but you should use some ideas of your own. Use the topic vocabulary feature to help you. Write 150–200 words.

Summary 8: My daughter can achieve whatever she wants

Topic vocabulary

Group A
disability
lost her feet

Group B
be fitted with
be measured for
prosthetic limb
artificial leg
cold to the touch

Group C
stare
make comments
unkind
teasing

Group D
hurt
upset
take to heart

Group E
reluctant to take part
give something a go
encourage
make a big difference

Group F
activities
sports
swimming
skiing

Group G
private treatment
specialist
orthopaedic centre

Group H
silicone
realistic-looking
match her exact skin tone

Group I
fund-raising event
sponsored event
donation
raffle

Group J
confidence
able to do anything

Vocabulary challenge 16

Distinguish between the following pairs of words and phrases taken from the vocabulary list above.

- *donation* and *raffle*
- *give something a go* and *reluctant to take part*

Writing task 16

On a visit to your local sports centre, you realise very few disabled people use the facilities. You believe the centre could do more to encourage their participation in sports. Write an email to the sports centre manager expressing these views. In your email you should mention:

- the length of time you have been a member
- what you enjoy about using the facilities
- why you think sport is for everyone, regardless of disability
- how the centre could encourage more people with disabilities to join.

Use the topic vocabulary feature to help you. Write 150–200 words.

....

....

Note-taking 9: The ugly side of clean power

Topic vocabulary

Group A
wind turbine
wind farm
wind power

Group B
level of noise
noise nuisance
reverberate
disturbing sounds
low thump

Group C
form of torture
put up with
cause constant stress
make people ill

Group D
electricity
renewable sources
power company
conventional power station

Group E
reduced air pollution
lower carbon emissions

Group F
countryside
coastline
skyline

Group G
low population
rural area
windy site
ugly landscape
eyesore

Group H
environmental cost
environmental group
campaign group
opposition group
concerned residents

Group I
break planning rules
government subsidies
developer

Group J
take advantage of
benefit from

Vocabulary challenge 17

Add the following words and phrases to the best three groups in the vocabulary list above. (They **are** taken from the text).

- vibration
- disrupt your sleep
- horizon

Writing task 17

There are plans to build a large recycling plant near where you live, to recycle glass, tins and paper. Write an email to your local newspaper saying whether or not you think this is a good idea. Here are some comments from your neighbours:

'The recycling plant will provide jobs in our area, which we need.'

'I hate the thought of the noise and the levels of pollution the plant will bring.'

'We all throw too much away – the recycling plant is part of our efforts to protect the environment.'

'The recycling plant is going to look so ugly and spoil an attractive landscape.'

The comments on page 98 may give you ideas but you should use some ideas of your own. Use the topic vocabulary feature to help you. Write 150–200 words.

Summary 9: From schoolboy to clown

Topic vocabulary

Group A
burning ambition
his dream came true
aspirations
love of the circus
thrilled at the prospect

Group B
begin training
talent
flair

Group C
clown
juggler
juggling
clubs
trapeze artist
perform in front of audience
clowning skills

Group D
dress up as
put on a performance
comedy routine
magic trick
fall over
mess up the act
roar with laughter

Group E
be made redundant
be offered work / a job
be promoted

Group F
home comforts
caravan
on tour
way of life

Group G
private tutor
one-to-one teaching
fall behind

Group H
exciting
marvellous
fantastic
agonising

Group I
soul-searching
decision-making

Vocabulary challenge 18

Add the following words and phrases to the best three groups in the vocabulary list above. (They are **not** taken from the text.)

- lose your job
- enjoyable
- study hard

Writing task 18

As a reward for completing exams, your school arranged for you and other school-leavers to visit a circus. Your headteacher would like to know if the visit to the circus was enjoyable and whether or not it should be repeated for next year's group.

You have been asked for your opinions. Here are some comments from your friends, giving their views:

'The clowns made us all roar with laughter.'

'The performances were disappointing. I have seen better magic tricks on television.'

'The atmosphere of the live audience was so exciting.'

'Some of the performers messed up their acts. Next year's group might prefer a concert.'

Write a report for the headteacher giving your views. The comments on page 100 may give you ideas but you should try to use some ideas of your own. Use the topic vocabulary feature to help you. Write 150–200 words.

Note-taking 10: The world of the Incas

Topic vocabulary

Group A
expedition
to excavate

Group B
remains of the old city
ruins
secrets of the past
world heritage site

Group C
historians
archaeologists

Group D
civilisation
culture
empire

Group E
engineering
architecture
astronomy

Group F
temples
palace
stone staircases
fountains

Group G
observatory
astronomers
star-gazing
planets

Group H
shrine
statue
to worship
to honour
solstices

Vocabulary challenge 19

Write a translation next to the words that you most want to remember. Check back in the text and use a dictionary if you need to.

Writing task 19

Your class recently visited the ruins of an ancient town. As you are a member of the history club, the headteacher has asked you to write a report about the visit. Here are some comments from your friends about the visit.

'The guide helped us understand how the town was built and what it looked like.'

'Old ruins are dull. I would have preferred to look at fantastic modern buildings.'

'We got information that will help us with our history exam.'

'There were not many signposts and some of us got lost.'

Write a report for the headteacher giving your views. The comments above may give you ideas but you should try to use some ideas of your own. Use the topic vocabulary feature to help you. Write 150–200 words.

....

....

....

....

Summary 10: What's for dinner, Mum?

Topic vocabulary

Group A
family meals
family mealtimes
family life
sit down to dinner
sit down together as a family
eat together

Group B
eat in front of the TV
grab a sandwich

Group C
delicious home cooking
huge platefuls
tasty
kitchen table
dinner table
serve dinner

Group D
rigid
strict
insist
insistent
expectations
disgruntled

Group E
row
quarrel
tell the children off
grumble
challenging
argumentative
conflict

Group F
lay the table
compliment the cook
civilised
intelligent discussion
enquire politely about

Group G
apron
saucepan
cookery book

Vocabulary challenge 20

Add the following words and phrases to the best three groups in the vocabulary list above. (They are **not** taken from the text.)

- oven
- pleasant conversation
- fight

Writing task 20

Are family meal times outdated in modern society or are they a tradition worth keeping? Here are some comments made by your classmates:

'We rarely sit down to a family meal as we are so busy with other activities.'

'A family meal makes us feel like a family – I love them.'

'It's not fair to expect mum or dad to make dinner when they've been working all day. We heat up a microwave meal if we're hungry.'

'Dinnertime is an important time when we all meet and share the news of the day.'

Write an article for a teenage magazine giving **your** views on the issue. The comments above may give you ideas but you should use some ideas of your own. Use the topic vocabulary feature to help you. Write 150–200 words.

Note-taking 11: Birth of a barcode

Topic vocabulary

Group A
Morse code
to convey messages
to scan
a barcode format

Group B
to commission products
to track products
management of stock
an efficient service

Group C
new product lines
a wider range of products
more variety of goods

Group D
computer technology
a laser scanner

Group E
family-run grocery store
retailers
food manufacturers

Group F
obstacles to overcome
a barrier to success

Group G
to lose custom
to become less profitable

Group H
the trend
the invention
the innovation

Group I
a vision
a dream

Vocabulary challenge 21

Extend three or four of the word groups in the vocabulary list above by adding **one** suitable word or phrase.

Writing task 21

Recently your school arranged for your class to have two weeks of work experience in a large supermarket. As class representative, you have been asked whether you would recommend work experience in a supermarket for next year's group. Here are some comments from your classmates about their experiences:

'In only two weeks, I learned so much about how a supermarket is organised.'

'Scanning products at the checkout was boring.'

'I enjoyed doing a wide variety of tasks.'

'It is definitely not my dream job. I want to do something fun and challenging.'

Write a report for the careers teacher giving your views. The comments above may give you ideas but you should try to use some ideas of your own. Use the topic vocabulary feature to help you. Write 150–200 words.

....

....

Summary 11: Pupils find internet 'a poor learning tool'

Topic vocabulary

Group A
traditional method
educational method
learning method
learning tool
current trend
present fashion

Group B
classroom activities
take notes from the teacher
use the internet
watch videos
contact with the teacher
do practical work
listen to explanations
group work

Group C
government-funded survey / study
commission research
report findings / results

Group D
rate as useful
value highly
rank poorly
effective
moderately enjoyable

Group E
information and communications technology (ICT)
multimedia approach
e-learning
CD-ROM
put the curriculum online

Group F
access to the internet
important resource

Group G
gather around a terminal
look at a monitor

Group H
concentrate
mess around

Group I
pupil
classmate
headteacher
textbook
computer

Vocabulary challenge 22

Add the following words and phrases to the best three groups in the vocabulary list above. (They **are** taken from the text.)

- answer questions
- distract others
- opinion

Writing task 22

Your headteacher is reviewing the use of the internet in your school. For two weeks she stopped all access to the internet for students. The headteacher would like to know how students felt about not having the internet for two weeks. She has asked you, as a member of the school computer club, to write a report. Here are some comments from your friends, giving their views:

'It didn't bother me. I prefer to take notes from the teacher and use library books.'

'Without the internet, I couldn't find the information I needed for my projects.'

'We soon got used to it. It was fun discussing our ideas together rather than going online.'

'The internet, especially social media, gives us so much, we were miserable without it.'

Write a report for the headteacher. The comments on page 108 may give you ideas but you should use some ideas of your own. Use the topic vocabulary feature to help you. Write 150–200 words.

Note-taking 12: Thirsty work

Topic vocabulary

Group A
fresh water
water supply
supply of clean drinking
  water
running water
water shortage
scarce

Group B
build a well
maintain
mend / fix

Group C
unsafe to drink
contaminated
polluted
untreated sewage
dangerous chemicals

Group D
diarrhoea
sap your energy

Group E
long-term
sustainable

Group F
implement a scheme
improve dramatically
water management
  policies
awareness-raising
  campaign

Group G
responsible water use
conserve water
leave the tap running
bucketful of water

Group H
developing country
the whole community

Vocabulary challenge 23

Add the following words and phrases to the best three groups in the vocabulary list above. (They **are** taken from the text). Then choose one of them and write a sentence to show its meaning.

- do repairs
- dirty water
- dehydration

Writing task 23

You have noticed people in your area being very careless in the way that they use water. You are concerned about this and decide to write an email to your local newspaper outlining your views. In your email, you may wish to include such things as:

- why water is so important
- examples of people wasting water
- problems the lack of clean water can cause
- how we could teach people, especially children, to respect water.

Use the topic vocabulary feature to help you. Write 150–200 words.

....

....

....

Summary 12: Lost for words

Topic vocabulary

Group A
local language
endangered
threatened by
under threat
in danger of being lost
in peril
die out
slip away

Group B
preserve
cling to
pass on

Group C
first language
mother tongue

Group D
ancestry
cultural heritage
contact with the past
wealth of memories
traditional skills
nomad

Group E
gossip
small talk
lilting
expressive

Group F
image problem
uncool
reject

Group G
inspiration
inspire

Vocabulary challenge 24

Add the following words to the best three groups in the vocabulary list above. (They are not taken from the text.)

- saying
- way of life
- motivate

Writing task 24

In many countries, the number of people speaking English as a second or additional language is increasing. Experts believe this trend will continue. How far do you think the spread of the English language is a positive development? Here are some comments made by young people:

'In my view, it's sensible to have a world language such as English because it makes international communication easier.'

'I see it as a negative trend. The spread of English is making other languages less important.'

'I don't mind – we can still use our first language whenever we want to.'

'If people want a good job they think learning English is a priority. Then children don't want to study their own language or literature properly.'

Write an article for your local newspaper giving **your** views about the spread of the English language across the world. The comments above may give you ideas but you should use some ideas of your own. Use the topic vocabulary feature to help you. Write 150–200 words.

Acknowledgements

The authors and publishers acknowledge the following sources of copyright material and are grateful for the permissions granted. While every effort has been made, it has not always been possible to identify the sources of all the material used, or to trace all copyright holders. If any omissions are brought to our notice we will be happy to include the appropriate acknowledgement on reprinting.

'Tackling dyslexia' by Judy Hobson, Health writer from Choice Magazine, adapted and used with permission from the author; 'The enemy within' by Emily Moore, (adapted) from Guardian Education © Guardian News & Media; 'Seeing cetaceans' by Anna Levin (adapted) from Immediate Media Company London Limited © BBC Wildlife Magazine/Immediate Media; 'Why zoo cats lose their cool' by Betsy Mason, (adapted) from New Scientist limited via Tribune Content Agency; 'A natural antiseptic' by Charlotte Baxter (adapted) © The Lady Magazine; 'The rose, the queen of all flowers' by Rob Boeck (adapted), from Horus, the in-flight magazine of Egypt Air; 'Sweet talk' by Linda Dell (adapted) © The Lady Magazine; 'Trolley to the tropics' by Phil Gates from Immediate Media Company London Limited © BBC Wildlife Magazine/Immediate Media; 'Gum and bananas: how Louise survived on a mountain' by David Fickling (adapted) © Guardian News & Media 2017; 'Young ambassadors' by Nikki Cooper © Guardian News & Media 2017; 'Gap years' by Jo Upcraft (adapted) from The Daily Telegraph © Telegraph Group London 2000; 'My daughter can achieve whatever she wants from Best magazine' © The National Magazine Company/Hearst Magazines UK; 'Ugly side of clean power' by Alexander Garrett © Guardian News & Media 2017; 'School boy to clown' by Richard Barber (adapted) © Sainsbury's Magazine 2002; 'What's for tea, Mum?' By Daphne Lockyer © Time Inc. (UK) Content and Brand Licensing; 'Pupils find internet a poor learning tool' by Julie Hendry, from The Sunday Telegraph © Telegraph Group London 2003; 'Lost for words' by David Newnham (adapted) from The Times Educational Supplement.

Thanks to the following for permission to reproduce images:

Cover Noppawat Tom Charoensinphon/Getty Images; Chapter 1 BSIP/Universal Images Group Editorial/GettyImages; Monty Rakusen/Cultura/GettyImages; Zinkevych/iStock/Getty Images Plus/GettyImages; parinyabinsuk/iStock/Getty Images Plus/GettyImages; Chapter 2 Schaef1/iStock/Getty Images Plus/GettyImages; Universal Images Group/GettyImages; Rubberball/Mike Kemp/GettyImage; Gabrielle Therin-Weise/Photographer's Choice RF/GettyImages; Chapter 3 JTB Photo/Universal Images Group/GettyImages; Mark Winwood/Dorling Kindersley/GettyImages; John Coletti/AWL Images/GettyImages; fcafotodigital/iStock/Getty Images Plus/GettyImages; Lucille Kanzawa/Moment/GettyImages; Chapter 4 Rahmat Marley/EyeEm/GettyImages; Jacob Ammentorp Lund/iStock/Getty Images Plus/GettyImages; Design Pics Inc/Alamy Stock Photo; John Giustina/The Image Bank/GettyImages; Chapter 5 DavidCallan/E+/GettyImages; Peter Muller/Photonica/GettyImages; Sura Ark/Moment/GettyImages; bowdenimages/iStock/Getty Images Plus/GettyImages; Chapter 6 Steve Debenport/E+/GettyImages; Juice Images/GettyImages; Barry Lewis/Corbis Historical/GettyImages; Cultura RM Exclusive/Philip Lee Harvey/Cultura Exclusive/GettyImages; Chapter 7 Paul Fearn/Alamy Stock Photo; hadynyah/E+/GettyImages; Bill Pugliano/Getty Images North America/GettyImages; Westend61/GettyImages; Chapter 8 Bettmann/GettyImages; Panoramic Images/GettyImages; Ken Ishii/Getty Images AsiaPac/GettyImages; Encyclopaedia Britannica/UIG/Universal Images Group.